Numeracy for QTLS

Numeracy for QTLS

Liz Keeley-Browne and Anne Price

Longman
is an imprint of

Harlow, England • London • New York • Boston • San Francisco • Toronto
Sydney • Tokyo • Singapore • Hong Kong • Seoul • Taipei • New Delhi
Cape Town • Madrid • Mexico City • Amsterdam • Munich • Paris • Milan

Pearson Education Limited
Edinburgh Gate
Harlow
Essex CM20 2JE
England

and Associated Companies throughout the world

Visit us on the World Wide Web at:
www.pearson.com/uk

First published 2011

ISBN: 978-1-4058-7354-3

British Library Cataloguing-in-Publication Data
A catalogue record for this book is available from the British Library

Library of Congress Cataloging-in-Publication Data
A catalog record for this book is available from the Library of Congress

10 9 8 7 6 5 4 3 2 1
15 14 13 12 11

Typeset in 9.5/12.5 pt Palatino by 73
Printed by Ashford Colour Press Ltd., Gosport

This book is dedicated to our colleagues and all other teachers/trainers who inspire the love of numeracy in those they teach.

Brief contents

Contents

Part 2 Tools of the trade

4 Numeracy in the curriculum   39

5 You and your learners   47

6 Some ideas and preparation for the tests   61

Part 3 Number competence

Preface

Welcome to *Numeracy for QTLS*. In writing this text the authors have a number of aims in mind. Our first and possibly most ambitious aim is to help you to become a competent and confident user of number, able to encourage and support your learners in the effective use of number. We intend to demonstrate the significant part number plays in our everyday lives and help you develop innovative and creative ways of using number with your learners.

We believe that numeracy can be fun. We are also aware that many of your learners will need support with numeracy skills. Numeracy competence is often linked to confidence and the realisation of its importance in everyday living. In this text our aim is to support you in making number relevant for your learners. We have offered exercises and activities to help you grow in confidence as teachers while at the same time offering example activities for use with your learners. We ardently believe that learning for a purpose is much more meaningful than learning imposed without explanation. As teachers ourselves we can quote the names of many students who became much more 'switched on' to numeracy when it gained a purpose.

It is important to remember too that skills in numeracy are crucial to the success of your learners and their employment prospects. In terms of national government priorities, competence in numeracy is essential to the country's ambition to be a world leader by 2020 and vital for survival in a competitive global world.

So, by the end of this book we hope that you will have learned to love number as we do, have come to understand the patterns and sequences that make number activities fun to do and, more important, will be able to enthuse your students to use number with confidence and with a real purpose.

Who should use this book?

The book is intended for use by all practitioners working in the Lifelong Learning sector and those intending to join this profession whether it be for a few hours a week or in a full-time role. It is for those new to teaching and training and those already practising in the sector who are now required to complete professional qualifications to demonstrate their 'fitness to practise' (DfES, 2006).

We also hope that the book proves useful for the experienced and qualified practitioner and would recommend particular sections in Chapter 4 and Chapter 6 which offer up-to-date advice on the changing requirements of the curriculum.

In this book we offer ideas for teaching numeracy as an integrated element of the vocational curriculum, we discuss the introduction of changes to the secondary curriculum and we offer exemplar tasks illustrating just how easy it is to practise and assess numeracy within a range of vocational contexts.

Structure of the book

The text divides naturally into three parts. In Part 1 we focus on 'barriers to learning', demonstrating the impact poor numeracy skills can have on life chances. The authors are aware of resistance by some to the inclusion of numeracy as an important and significant part of the training curriculum for teachers in the Lifelong Learning sector, and this issue is confronted, discussed and challenged. We are aware that some readers will be excited by the use of number but we also know that others will fear it. Our task is to identify the importance and extent of number use, to build your confidence in using it and, where necessary, to encourage you to incorporate number use into your teaching.

Part 2 continues to make the case for numeracy, providing support for your personal numeracy needs. Here we explore the number curriculum particularly in association with the current reforms to the 14–19 qualification framework. You will be encouraged to consider the numeracy requirements of your work role through a self-evaluation. After evaluating your personal skills you will be encouraged to complete an Individual Learning Plan to support the development of your personal numeracy skills. Having required you to assess your personal learning skills and abilities, Chapter 5 focuses on your learners and how you can best support them. The final chapter in this section develops further our philosophy of number teaching, advocating the teaching of numeracy through its application in real-life contexts. Here you will find ideas for teaching number concepts and for planning your session activities using actual and potential work situations which demand number competence. The approaches modelled here are learner centred, involve active learning and problem-based approaches within a framework which supports team working and assessment methodologies that encourage learning.

It is in Part 3 of the book where we begin to look at specific areas of numeracy both in terms of developing inclusive strategies for learners with numeracy needs and in the exploration of your own personal numeracy skills.

How to use the materials provided

Each chapter contains an introduction setting the scene for what is to follow with a rationale for its inclusion. Specific components of the numeracy minimum core as covered in each chapter will be identified. The standards addressed for those completing a training qualification are listed at the end of each introductory paragraph to enable those completing the tasks to use some of the evidence generation to support their full qualification ambitions. In this text we do not set out to cover all elements of the minimum core, but we do aim to demonstrate just how much can be covered in an integrated and interesting way. So, to be clear, this is not a textbook for Maths teachers delivering high-level qualifications. It is a book that tackles the issues and practical approaches associated with an integrated and problem-solving approach to number. Tasks will be set to encourage greater engagement and confidence. A 'self-evaluation' section will support the reader in exploring how number ability might influence their learners. The main teaching points of each chapter will be summarised and self-assessment exercises introduced to support the numeracy skills of those using this text as an aid to improving or refreshing their personal engagement with number.

And finally...

We hope you will enjoy reading this book, have fun playing with the ideas presented and make good use of it as a text to support you in your professional role as a competent and effective teacher/trainer in the Learning and Skills sector.

Acknowledgements

To our respective sons, daughter and husbands

Publisher's acknowledgements

We are grateful to the following for permission to reproduce copyright material:

Figures and tables
Figure 3.1: From Oxfordshire Connexions (www.spired.com/connexions), © 2010 Oxfordshire County Council; Figures 8.1 and 8.2: Courtesy of Microsoft Corporation; Figure 10.1: Copyright © 2008 Mark Reeve Animation Engineering (www.markreeve. co.uk/armature-r101-pic.html); Table 11.1: From Joint Council for Qualifications (www.jcq.org.uk); Figures 12.1, 12.2, 12.3 and 12.4: Courtesy of Microsoft Corporation.

Photos, cartoons and logos
Page 10: 'Skill' Logo from National Bureau for Students with Disabilities (www.skill. org.uk/index.aspx); Page 13: Advert from Gremlins campaign from Department for Education and Skills 9 (www.education.gov.uk). © Crown copyright 2010; Page 31: Cartoon from East Read: Welcome to Skill leaflet, CHANGE Picture Bank; Pages 80, 83, 106, 111, 112, 115: Images courtesy of Anne Price.

In some instances we have been unable to trace the owners of copyright material, and we would appreciate any information that would enable us to do so.

Part 1   BARRIERS TO LEARNING

This part identifies many of the barriers experienced by learners when working with number and poses some possible solutions for consideration by lecturers/trainers when working with learners who disengage from or avoid the use of number.

1 Confronting the issues

The area covered by this chapter is:

The influence different social and personal factors have on the development of numeracy skills.

In this chapter we explore attitudes to number and in so doing identify different learning journeys that bring us to the positions, prejudices and fears we may hold today. By the end of this chapter you will be able to demonstrate knowledge and understanding of the impact of learners' background on their approach to number. This chapter explores the factors that affect individual competency, ability and enthusiasm for number. The issues raised relate to young and adult learners alike.

The standards from the agreed competencies required of those training to teach in the Learning and Skills sector addressed in this chapter are:

AS 1, AS4, AK 1, AK 3

This chapter relates to the following minimum core standards for numeracy:

A1 Awareness of the range of personal, social and cultural factors including attitudes in the wider society, age, motivation, gender, ethnicity and socio-economic status in relation to numeracy

KEY WORDS: dyspraxia   dyscalculia   Maths phobia

Starting points

It is inevitable that early experiences of number influence the way individuals feel about it in later life. With this in mind we start with you, the trainee teacher, and pose a number of questions:

- Do you consider yourself competent and confident when using number?
- Why might Maths as a subject create more anxiety than other subject domains?
- How useful is it to ask learners to reflect on their prior experience with number?

The task places you in the position of being a learner again.

Task 1.1

Reflect on your experience of learning number.

- Would you define yourself as anxious, confident or somewhere between the two?
- Can you identify the factors that determine your perceptions?

In thinking about your experiences it is beneficial to go back as far as you can remember to the point at which you first started to acquire your numeracy skills.

Task 1.2

Think about your early experiences of learning number.

- Do you remember any toys or games you owned as a child that required the use of number?
- How did you learn to count, to recognise number form and shape?
- Can you remember any popular songs encouraging number use?

Discuss your list with a colleague or study partner.

- How might the list of games and songs popular today differ from when you were young? Comment on your findings.

Tasks 1.1 and 1.2 have been designed to encourage you to think and talk about your personal experiences. Complete the task below as a starting point for your reflective diary or Individual Learning Plan (explained below), describing your earliest memories of working with number, your successes, hopes and fears.

The Individual Learning Plan

If you are using this text as part of a training programme you will have been introduced to the idea of keeping an Individual Learning Plan (ILP). If this is a new idea to you then please log on to the accompanying website, www.pearsoned.co.uk/qtls, for this text where you will find a copy of an ILP you can use. We explore the use of ILPs in Chapter 5 of this text.

> The Individual Learning Plan Tool learning resource is downloadable from: **www.pearsoned.co.uk/qtls**.

Task 1.3

Log into the ILP. Use one of the reflect spaces to record your experiences with using number.

- In which area are you personally competent?
- Where do you need help?
- What has shaped your views and attitudes concerning number use?

You may be anxious about the focus on numeracy in your training programme. Anxiety is a difficult thing to deal with and can exacerbate a problem. When anxious we do not always think clearly. We believe that confidence is a key component in numeracy and would encourage you to consider how best to instil confidence in your learners and with your peers.

Task 1.4

Think about something that makes you anxious. Share this with a peer if you are able. Identify the impact this fear has on your ability to think and function.

Poor basic skills

The Moser Report produced in 2000 (DfES, 2000) highlights particularly concerns about the 'intergenerational' effect of poor basic skills. The research underpinning the report outcomes supported the commonly accepted perception that, when parents have trouble with reading, writing or numeracy, it is more likely that their children will start with a similar disadvantage. Parents with limited basic skills are obviously less able to give their children support if they have problems.

Discussion point

When visiting my local swimming pool recently I heard a young child count the number of bicycles in the rack and report to his mother that there were three. She then noticed two more and asked the child how many bicycles he could now see. The answer given by this bright and vocal 3-year-old immediately was five. Now compare this with another parent and child rushing to the pool with no time for conversation and consider the following:

- How influential are early experiences and encouragements to use numeracy?
- Are ability and skill in number mainly influenced by natural ability or our early experience?

The role of adults

The Moser Report (DfES, 2000) also highlighted to what extent failure to address the skills needs of adults, particularly of parents and grandparents, as well as the very young, could have a major impact on attempts to improve the country's basic numeracy and literacy skills and undermine a national effort to improve the nation's skills in the core areas as set out in the government's national literacy and numeracy strategies.

Consider the case study below which lists the membership of an adult numeracy class held in an inner-city community centre.

Case study

Liz is a retired primary school teacher who works as a volunteer teacher at her local community centre teaching basic numeracy skills on a Tuesday morning. In her class she has the following learners:

- Two female parents of young children wanting to improve their numeracy skills so that they can help their children.
- One ex-offender trying to improve his numeracy skills.
- Three males, new to working in the UK with second-language learning difficulties, competent at number but unsure of the language issues.
- One part-time firefighter who cannot pass the examinations to become a full-time employee and who lacks confidence in using number.
- One aspiring childminder who seeks social services approval to be a childminder and needs to demonstrate a certain level of numeracy ability to be accepted for the official Childminder register.

The individuals above, with their personal reasons for attending a numeracy class, represent a small sample of the adult population who in some way or other find their lack of number ability debilitating and limiting in their efforts to achieve their full potential.

Task 1.5

Consider the individuals identified above. What are the barriers that have impacted on their number learning and what factors have motivated them to take action?

There are some very real reasons why numeracy is so difficult for some people. We explore below some of the real and perceived reasons why numeracy for some is such a barrier. The first we identify is classified as Maths phobia.

Maths phobia

Rather difficult to diagnose and possibly something that many people suffer from to one degree or another is a condition we name Maths phobia. You may wish to consider how quickly you reach for a calculator to do simple sums. Do you trust your number work or do you ask someone else to check it? Have you developed strategies to avoid using number by perhaps asking someone else in the family to deal with financial issues? How often do you shy away from dealing directly with issues that require a competence in number?

Understanding how number works is an important part of everyday life from managing your money, travelling to work, shopping, paying bills or organising holidays. Below you will see the work of two groups of teacher trainees asked to explore the problems they have experienced with learning Maths. The two groups, identified as Groups A and B have identified a range of issues; some you may consider minor, others more significant, but nonetheless important to the individuals concerned. We have presented them as blocks which together can create a major hurdle for a Maths-phobic student.

Task 1.6

Review the material offered by Groups A and B in Figure 1.1 on page 8. Do you identify with any of the points raised? Did you experience concerns when learning Maths? Consider what each of the issues might mean to you as a teacher supporting learners who may suffer from Maths phobia.

A solution?

The section below provides a view as to how teachers should approach learners with Maths phobia. Do you agree with the views expressed? What strategies will you adopt to support learners with Maths phobia?

Task 1.7

Consider Maths phobia and the Helping diagram in Figure 1.2 on page 9.

- Do you agree with the issues raised by Groups A and B (Figure 1.1) and, more important, what do you think about the solutions offered (Figure 1.2)? Will you adopt these strategies in your teaching?

In your reflective learning log make notes of the key learning points for you arising from engaging with this activity.

Difficulties in dealing with number

There are recognised physical difficulties that may affect the development of numeracy skills. Here we mention briefly just a few commonly acknowledged difficulties namely: *dyspraxia* and *dyscalculia*.

Group A

Those who are good at Maths show off about it and make the rest of us feel incompetent.	When we did group work the boys were quicker, so we let them do it. It was not considered feminine or advisable to be better than the boys.	The teacher assumed we all knew exactly what he was doing. I was usually lost after about two minutes and too afraid to say anything for fear of holding up the whole class.

The cross symbol when I was wrong made me feel a failure. I often had a page of crosses and I didn't know why.	In some subjects you can do something and get some marks just by remembering a few facts, but in Maths it is very easy to get everything wrong.

It was like learning a whole new language with symbols and new words.	Some people can do it, some can't. I can't do Maths because I just don't understand it.	If you understand number you are in a special club. If you can't get the first bit right then it is best just to give up.

Group B

Girls can't do Maths anyway, so why should I bother?	I used to dread Maths lessons and spent most of the time just guessing at the answers.	All I remember about Maths at school was working through exercises and getting them wrong.
I bought myself a 'Teach Yourself Maths' book to help me pass my GCSE. No one else showed me how to do it.	So much depends on the teacher realising that some people just don't understand.	Saying 'Don't worry' immediately suggests it is your fault and everyone else can do it.

When teachers repeated their explanations I became even more confused. A new approach was needed.	Whenever the teacher said 'Don't worry' I felt even more of a fool.

I used to avoid being asked questions, which led to eventual exposure. I spent most Maths lesson, in absolute fear of detection.	It is like learning a new language, e.g. 'inverse of a matrix'. If you don't know what the words mean then you can easily become lost.	I was put in the wrong grade at school and found it all too hard, so I gave up.

Figure 1.1 Maths phobia

● Dyspraxia

The word 'dyspraxia' comes from the Greek words 'dys' meaning impaired or abnormal and 'praxis', meaning action or deed. Dyspraxia is considered a developmental disorder affecting initiation, organisation and performance of activities. Referred to as

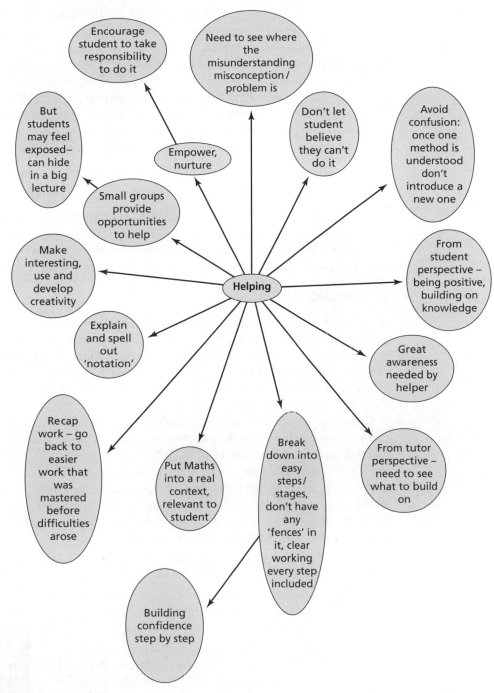

Figure 1.2 Helping

developmental coordination disorder (DCD) in the United States, it is a lifelong condition that is more common in males than in females. The exact proportion of people with the disorder is unknown, since the disorder can be difficult to detect owing to a lack of specific laboratory tests, making diagnosis of the condition one that first requires the elimination of all other possible causes/diseases. Current estimates of impact range between 5 and 20 per cent of the population suffering with the disorder with at least 2 per cent of these being affected severely. Some researchers believe that dyspraxia is not caused by a general medical condition, but may be the result of an immature neuron development. Dyspraxia is described as having two main elements:

1 *Ideational dyspraxia* – difficulty with planning a sequence of coordinated movements.

2 *Ideo-Motor dyspraxia* – difficulty with executing a plan even though it is known.

If you suspect one of your learners is suffering from dyspraxia, we suggest you talk to him/her and advise they seek support. There will be learning support advisors and specialists in most educational establishments specially trained to organise diagnosis and offer bespoke learning tips and approaches to support learners in dealing with their difficulties.

● Dyscalculia

Scientists at University College London (UCL) have shown that *dyscalculia* (or *number blindness*) is a biological reality. Their research has proved that, when shown a series of mathematical sums, some individuals experience the stifling condition of 'number blindness' brought about by a chemical reaction in the right parietal lobe. This chemical reaction has been observed in laboratory tests but it is still not clear why certain individuals experience such a response.

The researchers believe that dyscalculia is much like dyslexia (letter blindness) and affects up to one in twenty people. However, dyscalculia is often not recognised. The lead researcher for the project at UCL, Dr Roy Cohen Kadosh (UCL Institute for Cognitive Neuroscience), has discovered that stimulation to this brain region during a Maths test radically impacted on the subjects' reaction time. He claims his research provides strong evidence that dyscalculia is caused by malformations in the right parietal lobe of the brain. The research is seen as groundbreaking in supporting better understanding of those who experience problems with numeracy.

> It's an important step to the ultimate goal of early diagnosis, which in turn will lead to earlier treatments and more effective remedial teaching.   (*Journal of Current Biology*: March, 2007)

If you wish to explore the topic of dyscalculia further we recommend you explore the work of Trott, particularly the articles referenced below.

> **Trott, C.** (2003) 'Mathematics Support for Dyslexic and Dyscalculic Students', *Journal of the Professional Association of Teachers of Students with Specific Learning Difficulties*, 16(2), pp. 22–28.

> **Trott, C.** (2005) 'Maths Support for an Engineering Student with Dyslexia', *Working with Students with Disabilities, LTSN Engineering, 2nd ed.*, pp. 28–9 (ISBN 1904190170).

Should these difficulties prove insurmountable, then Skill: National Bureau for students with Disabilities, should be contacted, www.skill.org.uk/teaching.

Source: Skill. Used with permission

If you are interested in reading more about the impact of learning difficulties on an individual's potential capacity to learn, then see Chapter 10 in *Training to Teach in the Learning and Skills Sector* by Liz Keeley-Browne (one of the authors of this text), also published by Pearson Education.

Help with number

As a result of national concern about poor levels of numeracy skill, the government has funded the development of a special programme of diagnostic and developmental tools to help people overcome their number fears. The 'Move On' programme commissioned by the Learning and Skills Improvement Service offers a direct approach to the promotion, engagement and delivery of number training, highlighting opportunity for all rather than need for some. It describes the benefits that learning and qualifications can bring and encourages people to believe in their ability to improve progress. The materials available at **www.move-on.org.uk** are accessible, user friendly and supportive.

The Move On site contains the following sections:

- **Promotion**. Offering the opportunity to improve maths skills. The focus is on gaining qualifications and progressing rather than on people's problems and needs. The language then asks 'Would a maths qualification help you to move on?' rather than being couched in the negative voice as 'Have you got problems with your reading, writing and maths?'

- **Engagement**. This section offers training and tools for use in a community context, in education and in the workplace and is designed for those who have frequent contact with potential learners. The training gives an opportunity to explore the use of positive language and try your skills out with a National Test.

- **Delivery**. Here you can access a number of focused learning opportunities offering a chance to develop skills and achieve a national qualification, which enables learners to:
  - develop wider skills
  - prepare and practise their skills in order to take the National Tests in Numeracy, when ready.

The Move On Learner Route provides opportunities for online skills development and practice tests.

Task 1.8

Log on to the Move On website.

- Access the section on tests.
- Complete the test and receive the diagnostic analysis of your skill level.
- Copy the result and place it in your Individual Learning Plan.

Have you reached the appropriate level? What do you need to do next in order to 'Move On'?

If the test has identified that your numeracy skills are below Level 2, then you need to complete an Action Plan to ensure that your personal numeracy ability improves during your training period. The Move On website can help you to improve your skills and prepare you gradually for the next time you need to sit the tests. Perhaps you are 'rusty' and just need practice and more confidence. You may need more help than the Move On site can provide; if this is the case discuss your needs with your tutor.

Place your Action Plan in your ILP folder.

You may have found the Move On tests more difficult than you expected. If this is the case *we recommend you seek help immediately*. This is a really difficult thing to do as a trainee teacher and requires a great deal of courage.

The following section offers you information on where and how to gain advice and support. You will need to read for your personal needs but also to know how to advise your students.

The educational institution where you are studying will have additional support advisors to help you. Do contact them. Very few individuals are skilled in everything they try to do and we can all benefit from extra support from time to time. If, however, you are reluctant to talk to staff who may work in the same organisation as you do, then email 'read.write.plus' at **rwp.excellencegateway.org.uk**. The site logo is shown below.

You may well be familiar with the now famous gremlin Get On campaign as part of the government's Skills for Life strategy, which aims to help 2.25 million learners gain a qualification by 2010. The campaign using the gremlin character was launched in 2001 specifically to target the millions of people with literacy, numeracy and language needs.

A testimonial advocating the benefits of the campaign is reproduced below:

The highly successful novelist, Philip Escoffey, whose novels include *Bravo Two Zero* and the Quick Reads® book *The Grey Man*, commented:

'I know better than most what it's like to be in hiding, but not many people realise that I was undercover in more ways than one. I struggled with reading and writing until I entered the army, and it was only once I had the support of excellent adult learner tutors that I was able to take on my gremlins, win the battle and develop new skills. Just look where improved writing skills have got me! It might seem daunting at first, but I call upon anyone who feels assaulted by their gremlins to make a change for the better and call the Get On campaign on 0800 66 0800. You'll be better equipped once you've talked to someone who can recommend free local courses.' *(rwp.excellencegateway.org.uk)*

Task 1.9

What is your opinion of the gremlin campaign? Does this approach really work? If you were designing an advert recommending reluctant learners to engage in numeracy training what approach would you adopt?

Advice for the number averse

One possible cure for Maths phobia is to allow a few numbers back into your life by adopting the following strategies:

1 Recognise that you have an aversion to maths whether it's full-blown Maths phobia or just a few maths blocks here and there.

2 Make a conscious decision to do something about it.

3 Give yourself a regular maths workout, however small to start with.

Try the exercises at the end of each chapter in this book. Monitor your progress.
    Number workout in 25 seconds of mental arithmetic – start the time.

Number workout

Time yourself if you want to know whether you improve in speed as well as accuracy by the time you reach the end of the book. Questions become more challenging as you progress through the exercise.

1.1
a. 11 + 39 − 40
b. 111 + 389 − 400
c. 1111 + 3889 − 4000

1.2

a. 41 + 28 − 40

b. 111 + 28 − 37

c. 111 + 28 − 41

1.3

a. 24 + 17 − 12 + 16

b. 69 + 23 − 47 + 15

c. 111 + 56 − 87 + 14

Record in your portfolio how long it took you to complete this exercise. Did you need to use a calculator or were you able to complete all three sums in your head? What number strategies did you adopt to help you to succeed?

Summary

In this chapter you have been introduced to the following:

- Some of the medical conditions that can impact on an individual's ability to learn number.
- The damaging affects of numeracy both socially and financially.
- How to use an ILP.
- Three recognised number difficulties namely: dyspraxia, dyscalculia and Maths phobia.
- The fears of a group of teacher trainees and their ideas about how to address number competence in a learning environment.

Reflections on Chapter 1

- What have you gained from reading this chapter?
- Are you more aware now of some of the issues involved with teaching number?
- Do you need to develop your own skills and confidence in this important area of learning?

The political context

This chapter explores the political drivers that underpin the current focus on number competence. It gives summary presentation to the research that informs government thinking and shows the impact of poor numeracy skills on individual life chances.

By the end of this chapter you will be able to:

- Understand the policy framework that has underpinned the current focus on skills.
- Develop a critical awareness of the significance to the individual learner, the community and the national economy of numeracy development.

The standards from the agreed competencies required of those training to teach in the Learning and Skills sector addressed in this chapter are:

AS 1, AS4, AS7, CP 3, BP 3

This chapter relates to the following minimum core standards for numeracy:

A1 Awareness of the range of personal, social and cultural factors including attitudes in the wider society, age, motivation, gender, ethnicity and socio-economic status in relation to numeracy

KEY WORDS: **policy** **labour market** **globalisation**

Introduction

Concern about the UK global economic position led to the commissioning by government of what is commonly known as the Leitch Report (DfES, 2006). The report highlights research by the Organisation for Economic Co-operation and Development (OECD) which demonstrates that the UK is performing poorly in terms of training a population with the skills needed for twenty-first-century economic survival. To improve the UK's global position the optimal skill levels required for 2020 are likely to require 50 per cent increase in workers in highly skilled occupations.

As a result of the report, which also identified poor levels of achievement in basic skills, a number of initiatives have been launched to encourage greater skill level development. We discuss the curriculum driving this approach in Chapter 4 of this text.

Discussion point

- Are young people leaving school today equipped for the future?
- Have students leaving school been able to access jobs in the labour market?
- What types of work are the young interested in?
- In what industries have new job opportunities arisen and how important have numeracy skills been in gaining employment in this area?

Task 2.1

Reflect on your discussion; consider the essential nature of ability in core skills particularly those of numeracy. Record your thoughts in your ILP.

Technology changes

Greater use of technology has increased productivity in many areas. Government sources monitoring the impacts of technological change have identified falling barriers to trade, new markets and new technologies as providing a guaranteed way out of economic recession (DWP, 2008). In addition, research has shown (Felstead, 2009) that the skills required for twenty-first-century employment are changing from manual skills towards 'desk' skills, with a strong focus on ICT and numeracy. Productivity gains in 2009 have been strongly biased toward skilled occupations with high-skilled workers increasingly in demand and those with low skills finding themselves more likely to be unemployed.

Discussion point

Is the current labour market polarising between high- and low-skilled jobs and, if it is, are you aware of the consequences for people's opportunities to progress?

Task 2.2

Reflect on your discussion. Consider the essential nature of ability in core skills particularly those of numeracy. Record your thoughts in your ILP.

Task 2.3

What sort of skills are required in the sectors where employment is currently available in your locality?

2

Globalisation

The impacts of globalisation with lowering barriers to trade and the expansion of the global labour force will create new challenges and opportunities for the UK. The challenges relate specifically to greater competition in the labour market with the integration of China and India into the world economy (Freeman, 2005). These facts have led to fears of competition placing downward pressure on low-end wages and jobs in the UK as cheap goods and services are imported (DWP, 2009). OECD analysis suggests that 20 per cent of employment in Europe could be affected by outsourcing in the future (OECD, 2007).

The financial costs of poor number skills

Research carried out by the accountants KPMG monitoring a group of children with poor numeracy over a number of years found those with low numeracy skills were more likely to be unemployed, claim more benefits and pay less tax. The report demonstrates that poor numeracy skill often links to unemployment and the need for state support. KPMG estimate that children who are poor at Maths at school cost the taxpayer up to £2.4 billion on an annual basis. In addition, the report estimates that the long-term costs of children leaving school unable to do Maths could be as high as £44,000 per individual up to the age of 37. This research makes it apparent that basic numeracy skills are essential for individual success and for economic prosperity. This is why it makes good economic sense and is of course ethical to intervene to help people develop core numeracy skills.

Research carried out in 2006 for the Department for Work and Pensions clearly shows a correlation between the impact that levels of qualification have on an individual's employment prospects. The chart shows that the higher the level of qualification you hold, the greater is your likelihood of being employed. Those qualified to Level 5 or above are the most likely to be employed (at 89 per cent). However, only 48 per cent with no qualifications (less than half the population with no qualifications) were found to be in employment.

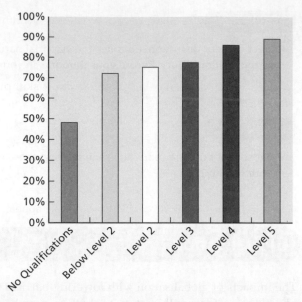

Figure 2.1 Percentage qualification by level for the UK population (2006)
Source: Data collected from Labour Force Survey Quarter 4:2006

Ability in numeracy has been linked very closely with potential earning power. Table 2.1, produced some time ago by the International Adult Literacy Society in the UK (IALS), illustrates the distribution of annual earnings for people with different levels of literacy and numeracy.

The data are old now. However, the table still reveals interesting patterns that highlight the significance of poor number skill. The table shows that 55 per cent of the population (26 + 29 per cent) with low levels of numeracy earn less than £15,000 a year whereas for literacy only 49 per cent (20 + 29 per cent) of the population fall in this low-paid earning bracket. The indications are that poor numeracy skills have a greater impact on earning power than do weaknesses in literacy.

Furthermore, a report produced for the Basic Skills Agency in 1997 entitled 'Does Numeracy Matter?' based on a sample of 37-year-old adults who all left school at 16

Table 2.1 Annual earnings

Annual earnings	Literacy		Numeracy	
	Low level	*High level*	*Low level*	*High level*
Up to £9,600	20	11	26	6
£9,601–£15,000	29	12	29	10
£15,001–£19,000	27	16	22	17
£19,001–£25,200	17	20	15	21
Over £25,201	7	40	7	46
Total	100	100	100	100

Source: Created from data provided by the International Adult Literacy Society (IALS) 1985, as part of Statistics Canada

found that, whereas 30 per cent of women with competent numeracy and low literacy earned below £150 per week, the percentage for women in the same income bracket with low numeracy and competent literacy was almost twice as high, at 58 per cent.

Here is undeniable evidence that poor numeracy skill impacts on earning power, and for women in particular poor numeracy skill plays a greater impact than do low levels of literacy.

Task 2.4

Discuss the implications of poor numeracy skills on the earning power of an individual. Why do you think that poor numeracy skills appear to create a greater disadvantage than deficiencies in literacy?

The minimum core and teacher-training requirements

As part of the strategy to increase the numeracy and literacy skills of the population, government strategy has focused on the Learning and Skills sector where a plethora of reforms has gradually transformed the way teachers are trained in this sector. The publication of *Success for All* (DfES, 2002) demonstrated a clear commitment to improving the quality of teaching and learning in the sector. The strategy to reform the sector was set out in a document entitled *Equipping our Teachers for the Future* (DfES, 2004) which outlined the introduction of new teacher training qualifications including a Diploma at Level 5 (New Qualification Framework), a Certificate qualification at Level 4 and a smaller one-unit qualification at Level 3 (for those teaching for limited times in a set period or studied as an introductory threshold qualification) named a PTLLS (Preparing to Teach in the Lifelong Learning sector).

In addition, a number of specific changes to teacher training have focused on numeracy skills. At the time of the publication of *Success for All* (2002) there was an expectation that initial teacher training courses should equip all trainee teachers with the knowledge and skills needed to develop inclusive approaches to addressing the literacy and numeracy needs of their learners (Blackstone, 2000). The Minimum Core (FENTO, 2003) reinforced this expectation and defined for the first time the personal literacy and numeracy skills required of teachers in the Lifelong Learning sector. From 2007 all trainee teachers have been required to demonstrate competence in literacy, numeracy and ICT as a requirement to be awarded qualified teacher status. The FENTO minimum core has also been revised and new standards approved for the design, delivery and assessment of the numeracy core as part of the total reform to the qualifications required of those teaching in the sector.

The twin concerns of government to ensure the professionalisation of all teachers in the Lifelong Learning sector and to place greater emphasis on the literacy and numeracy knowledge, understanding and skills of the teachers create a number of challenges for trainee teachers, teacher trainers and the already trained.

Task 2.5

Discuss the challenges created by the increased focus on numeracy in the training requirements of teachers for the Learning and Skills sector. Do you think it appropriate
that teachers should be required to demonstrate personal competence before being
admitted to the profession? If not, why not?

Policy implementation

An Ofsted Survey Inspection in 2003 found that 58 per cent of in-service Certificate in
Education/PGCE students had a GCSE Grade C or equivalent in English, while the
figure was 50 per cent for Mathematics. As a result, legislation was approved to require
the introduction of training in and assessment of a minimum core of language, literacy
and numeracy into teacher education programmes for the sector. This was achieved in
2004. This minimum core was revised and extended as part of the reform of teacher
education programmes in 2007 and ICT has now been included.

The minimum core should be covered in your training programmes through the
three units of assessment of the initial teacher education programmes that form part of
your study. The units of study are: Planning and Enabling Learning, Enabling Learning and Assessment, Theories and Principles for Planning and Enabling Learning. With
regard to the assessment of the minimum core, it was intended that knowledge and
understanding relating to literacy, language, numeracy and ICT should be assessed
internally by providers, while personal skills in English and Mathematics would be
assessed by external tests.

At the time of writing, it appears that these tests will not be implemented but
that those seeking Qualified Teacher Learning and Skills status (QTLS) and Associ-
ate Teacher Learning and Skills status (ATLS) would need to hold 'approved Level 2
qualifications in literacy/English and numeracy/Mathematics [which] will count as
proxy for the personal skills in literacy and numeracy as described in the minimum
core'. (LLUK, 2008:2).

There are two distinct but related issues pertinent to the consideration of the minimum core for trainee teachers. The first relates to knowledge, understanding and personal skills and requires acknowledgement of the minimum personal skills needed to
function effectively as a teacher in the sector.

Task 2.6

Consider the numeracy skills as described in *Addressing Literacy, Language, Numeracy and ICT Needs In Education and Training: Defining The Minimum Core of Teachers' Knowledge, Understanding and Personal Skills,* accessible at: **www.lluk.org/
documents/minimum_core_may_2007_3rd.pdf**.

● Which activities involved in your teaching role will require you to be a competent
   user of number?

The second issue regarding the minimum core requires decisions about how teaching and learning are delivered with there being some divergence of practice in terms of approaches being adopted in the sector. The extract below is from research carried out by the National Research and Development Centre for adult literacy and numeracy on embedding language, literacy and numeracy (LLN) in post-16 programmes and considers the features of teaching where this happens:

- Teaching is linked to practical, vocational content and activities.
- Materials are contextualised to the vocational area.
- Initial/diagnostic assessment contributes to the integration of numeracy into vocational teaching.
- There is differentiation according to needs in the way in which the vocational subject is taught.
- Numeracy is seen as essential in the development of learners' professional identity and for success in their vocational area.
- Numeracy development is treated in practice as relevant to all learners, not only necessary for those who are identified with LLN needs.

What this means in practice will vary from one curriculum area to another. For example, on a Health and Social Care course, the vocational teacher uses her own experience as a nurse and quotes real-life situations to demonstrate the importance of numeracy for such vocational tasks as measuring drugs. On an Entry/Level 1 Motor Vehicle course, the teaching, evidencing and assessment for numeracy are carried out in practical sessions in an automotive engineering workshop, and differentiated to three levels.

This approach, applied by competent and committed teaching staff, has a number of advantages as it allows the learners to appreciate the importance of numeracy competence in their working lives. It is the embedded approach to numeracy that we, the authors, would like to encourage in this text.   (Casey et al., 2006: 30–32)

Task 2.7

- How are LLN skills taught in your institution or training placement?
- Are they taught discretely or are they embedded into the vocational programme?
- Does this vary from one section/department to another or is there a whole institution policy/strategy?
- Discuss core skill delivery approaches with your colleagues and/or peers. What are the advantages and disadvantages of each approach?

Number workout

Time yourself if you want to know whether you improve in speed as well as accuracy by the time you reach the end of the book.

2.1
a. 5 × 4 × 2
b. 50 × 3 × 6
c. 500 × 9 × 2

2.2
a. 5 × 11 × 3
b. 15 × 6 × 8
c. 51 × 2 × 7

2.3
a. 7 × 6 × 3 × 4
b. 19 × 3 × 8 × 2
c. 67 × 5 × 3 × 2

Summary

In this chapter you have been introduced to the following:

- The policy context driving government concern about and investment in raising the skill level of the school and adult population.
- Data which demonstrate the significant financial benefit to society and the individual where proficiency in number can be demonstrated.
- The focus on the minimum core requirements in your teaching qualifications.

Reflections on Chapter 2

- What have you gained from reading this chapter?
- Are you more aware now of some of the issues involved with teaching number?
- Do you need to develop your own skills and confidence in this important area of learning?

3 Motivational and social factors

This chapter explores issues of motivation and considers the social factors influencing an individual's approaches to numeracy. Dimensions such as gender, ethnicity and disability affecting numeracy development are explored.

By the end of the chapter you will be able to:

- Consider the impact of learners' backgrounds and needs on numeracy learning.
- Discuss concepts and language associated with maths and number.

> *The standards from the agreed competencies required of those training to teach in the Learning and Skills sector addressed in this chapter are:*
>
> **AS 1, AS4, AS 7, CS 3, ES 3-6**

> *This chapter relates to the following minimum core standards for numeracy:*
>
> **A2** Begin to address the needs of learners with learning difficulties and disabilities and seek expert advice for specific learning needs

KEY WORDS: diversity refugee gender inclusive learning barriers to participation

Introduction

It is your responsibility as a trainee teacher to create the best possible learning environment for your learners even though external factors linked to time, space and place may well lie outside your control. External factors may militate against your efforts to secure an appropriate learning environment, but there are a number of components for effective learning within your control. For example, there are strategies you can apply to help learners engage positively with number. To do this it is important to be aware of the personal, social and cultural factors that impact on a learner's ability and attitude to number. This chapter highlights some barriers to learning, supports this with numerical evidence while also suggesting ways in which you might wish to gather similar evidence with your learners. Through exemplar activities we show how easy it is to integrate activities involving number into everyday learning experiences.

The impact on communities and society

A great deal of information is available concerning the social characteristics of people with poor basic skills levels. These have significant consequences for the capacity of local communities to regenerate, for democratic participation, for the criminal justice system, the public health agenda and for issues of social welfare.

Compared to those with adequate skills, adults with poor basic skills are:

- up to five times more likely to be unemployed or out of the labour market;
- more likely to live in a household where both partners are not in paid employment;
- more likely to have children at an earlier age, and to have more children;
- more likely to have children who also struggle with basic skills;
- less likely to own their own home;
- less likely to be in good health;
- less likely to be involved in public life, a community organisation or to vote;
- more likely to be homeless;
- over-represented in prisons and young offenders' institutions.

It Doesn't Get Any Better, Bynner and Parsons, 2006; *The basic skills of young adults*, Ekynsmith and Bynner, 1994; HM Prison Service, 1998.

Task 3.1

Consider a learner you have met in your work environment who experiences difficulty with number.

- Can you predict the likely outcome for him/her in terms of employment opportunities and future life experiences?

The NEET (Not in Education, Employment or Training)

The United Kingdom was the first country worldwide to use the classification for those not engaged in any training or employment as 'NEET'. Reducing the proportion of 16- to 18-year-olds in the NEET category is a priority for the government. Being identified as NEET between the ages of 16 and 18 is seen as a major predictor of later unemployment, low income, teenage motherhood, depression or poor physical health (DCSF website).

Being out of (not in) education, employment or training (NEET) between the ages of 16 and 18 is potentially an enormous waste of young people's potential and ability to contribute to society. What is more, being NEET is often linked to a number of other poor outcomes, including low levels of attainment, teenage conception and even early death.

Reducing the proportion of young people NEET is therefore one of the government's key national priorities. The target is to reduce the proportion of 16–18-year-olds who are NEET by two percentage points on an annual basis over the next five years. Local authorities have the lead responsibility for reducing the proportion of young people NEET in their areas. The latest figures show that 189,500 (9.4 per cent) of 16- to 18-year-olds were NEET at the end of 2007, a reduction from 210,000 (10.4 per cent) at the end of 2006. When broken down by age, the proportion of 16- to 17-year-olds NEET fell from 8.2 to 7.2 per cent in this period, and 18-year-olds NEET from 14.7 to 13.7 per cent.

Figure 3.1 shows the percentage of school pupils aged 16 in 2006/2007/8 in one county. The table shows destination data over three years in a range of groups including those remaining in school, those employed and the NEET category. The patterns here generally reflect the national picture with a reduction in the NEET. There is some differentiation in 2008, however, when the NEET category appears to show an increase on the previous year's figures.

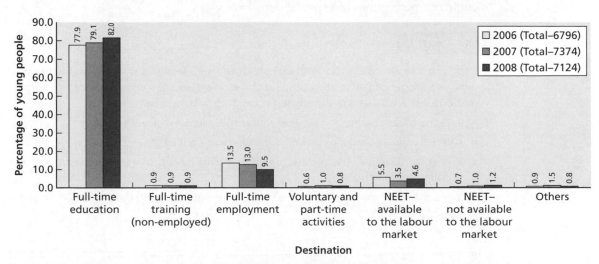

Figure 3.1 Year 11 leavers' destinations for 2006, 2007 and 2008, percentage comparison

Source: Connexions Direct, www.connexions-direct.com. Used with permission

25

Drawing on the data provided we can see that in 2006 77.8 per cent of 16-year-olds remained in full-time study with the figure rising to 82 per cent by 2008. The data are from one specific region. You may wish to explore more recent data from your own locality. It would be interesting to explore, for example, the impact of the recession on the data, and identify also regional differences in trends during any specific period.

Task 3.2

- Does your organisation have a strategy for early identification of potential NEET learners?
- What structures are in place to support those who may be exhibiting early signs of 'drop out'?

You may wish to access the Year 11 destination data for your region (contact your local authority) and interrogate the available data.

Factors affecting the acquisition and development of numeracy skills

In any group of people you will find a variety of expertise, interest and ability in relation to a range of matters. We all have different skills and aptitudes and these differences may be explained through a variety of ways. The ability to use number effectively is one of the most interesting areas to explore with any group. There are those who find number really difficult while others become fanatically obsessed and excited by number patterns, pictures and problems.

The exercise below is designed to investigate the views of a group of learners in relation to number work. Our interest here is in exploring views rather than skills and aptitudes although, of course, there is often a correlation between ability and enjoyment in our perceptions of a specific domain of work.

Task 3.3

Carry out a small-scale survey with a group of learners. Design a short questionnaire to explore age, gender, ethnicity (assuming group members are willing to share this information) and enthusiasm or otherwise for working with number.

Collect the data together and analyse your results. Summarise your findings.

- Did this exercise challenge any of your stereotypical views?
- Were, for example, the female members of the group more enthusiastic about number than the male?
- Were the more mature members of the class more interested than those under the age of 30?

The results of your mini-investigation will show that those participating in learning are not a homogeneous group. Further investigation is likely to reveal that within the group will be those who have felt demotivated through lack of confidence, disaffection or a feeling that it is not for them. You will also meet individuals who love to engage in learning but were unable to do so because of external barriers. As with the group you are working with, so it will be with your learners.

Barriers to participation

In your teaching you will meet students who experience barriers that stop them from learning. The barriers cited by non-learners usually fall into three distinct clusters:

- attitudinal, including confidence and motivation;
- physical and material, such as finance and time;
- structural, around the way education and training are provided.

Figure 3.2 shows the results of a small-scale survey carried out with a group of prospective teachers in training who did not have a Level 2 qualification on application to the course. Its purpose was to explore their attitudes to learning number. You may wish to carry out a similar survey with your colleagues and/or learners.

Task 3.4

Comment on the results in Figure 3.2. Are they as you would expect? Where do they differ?

● Attitudinal barriers

The results of your survey may be different. In the survey in Figure 3.2 lack of confidence in the individual's own ability to learn was seen as producing negative attitudes to education and training. Carry out the survey with different groups of learners. Your results may vary according to the age, ability and/or ethnicity of your sample group.

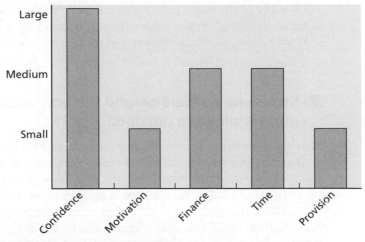

Figure 3.2 Attitudinal barriers to learning

Dench and Regan (2000) found that older learners offered lack of time as the main reason for not participating in numeracy learning. Younger learners felt there were no tangible benefits to be gained from engagement with numeracy learning. Here peer group association appeared to reinforce an anti-learning culture which some find difficult to overcome (McGivney, 1990).

● Physical and material barriers such as finance and time

Among the identifiable physical and material barriers are problems associated with time, affordable childcare, lack of information and geographical isolation. Consider the Case study presented below.

Case study

Ruth is a single mother who left school aged 14 with no qualifications. Her daughter is about to start school and Ruth would like to return to part-time education and study to become a classroom assistant. She has high ambitions eventually to obtain a Foundation degree.

There are a number of factors militating against her success:

- Her local college is seven miles and two bus changes away.
- Courses start at 9 a.m., just fifteen minutes after she is permitted to leave her daughter unattended at school.
- She thinks the course is free, but she has no spare income to pay a childminder or fund her travel.

Task 3.5

Are you aware of anyone who might wish to engage in more learning but who faces a number of challenges before they can begin to start the learning process? Describe the factors affecting their progress in your learning log and explore ways in which you might be able to offer advice and guidance to such learners.

● Structural barriers around the way education and training are provided

Structural barriers may group into areas associated with the availability of work-related training and, in the past, benefit disincentives. Learners who enrolled on a full-time course of training have in the past found their entitlement to social security benefits removed. The benefit system has now been revised and there are a number of fiscal measures in place to encourage the unemployed to engage in training. These include Train to Gain, a scheme introduced by the last government (Policy Exchange, 2010) and Apprenticeships.

More information is available from the following website: **www.directgov.gov.uk**.

Breaking down the barriers

It will be your role as a teacher to engage and enthuse people who do not have a strong learning track record. When it comes to working with number this is an area of particular challenge. You are likely to meet in your teaching groups learners with high numeracy competence and others who will avoid working with number. When teaching mathematical processes, it is important to be aware that every 'subject' has its own language of discourse. An understanding of this basic language is essential if your students are to become independent learners and have mastery and self-confidence in the use of number.

3

The language of number

Definition Football

This is a Game to test knowledge and understanding.

The success of the football (netball) match depends on serious training in preparation for the game. It will involve memorising the information on the card provided. Each team should be allocated copies of the information sheets.

1 Divide the class into two teams. Each team should appoint a captain.

2 Allow a period of time for learning the content of the information sheets and then ask for all books and notes to be put away.

3 Toss a coin to see who has kick-off and the game begins.

4 The team with kick-off receives the first question from the teacher/trainer. If a member of the team answers correctly within five seconds the team keep possession and a second question is asked. Again, if someone on this team answers correctly within five seconds, the ball is deemed to have passed successfully and possession is retained. Three correct answers (three passes) and it's a goal.

5 If a player answers incorrectly, that is a tackle and the question passes to the other team. If no one in that team can answer within five seconds it is classified as a loose ball. If the opposition can answer within five seconds they pick up possession and begin to receive questions.

6 Fouls are committed by shouting out answers when it's not your team's turn, for answering when you are ineligible and for arguing with the referee. Red and yellow cards can be employed.

The winning team is the one with more goals at the end of the session.

Number words and definitions for use with the above game include:

Evaluate: find or state the number or amount

Estimate: a rough calculation

Interpret: explain the meaning of

Solve: find an answer to

Percentage: a fraction with a denominator of 100, but written as the numerator followed by '%'

Proportion: a part or share that might be compared with another

Calculate: obtain a value for

Classify: arrange in categories

Compare: liken to, find similarities with

Function: a quantity that may change, expressed in terms of another

Analyse: examine, investigate

Symmetrical: capable of being divided into parts of equal shape and size

Perimeter: the total length or circumference of an enclosed shape

Triangle: a shape with three sides

Square: a shape with four equal sides and four right angles

Rectangle: a shape with two pairs of parallel sides and four right angles

Area: The measure of a total surface of a two-dimensional shape

Perimeter: the circumference or outline of a closed figure

Dissection: cutting into pieces

Circumference: the enclosing boundary of a circle

Radius: a straight line from the centre to the circumference of a circle or sphere

Cuboid: a three-dimensional shape, each side being a rectangle

Probability: the likelihood of an event occurring

Measure: a process of attributing a value to some attribute, e.g. length.

You will find a comprehensive list of terms used in numeracy on:
www.tda.gov.uk/skillstests/numeracy/glossary.aspx.

Task 3.6

- Consider how you might adapt the above activity for learners with learning difficulties or second-language acquisition needs.
- How can you help learners with limited understanding of the language of maths to improve their vocabulary and understanding?
- Consider how much language acquisition can impact on learners' ability to do maths.

Teaching new arrivals

Our teaching environments may contain students from a rich variety of backgrounds. Your class could potentially contain students form more than ten different nationalities, all with varying understandings of number and with different levels of language competence. Such diversity in the student body is both stimulating for you as a teacher but at the same time can be challenging. This situation occurs throughout the Western world.

In Western Europe, the number of students whose home language is different from the language spoken at school is rapidly increasing. The number of students who are not citizens of the country (generally referred to in Europe as 'foreigners') increased 26 per cent in Germany, 17 per cent in the Netherlands, and 11 per cent in Switzerland between the mid-1980s and early 1990s. During the same period, the number of students in Norway speaking a language other than Norwegian increased 136 per cent and the number in Sweden speaking a language other than Swedish increased 30 per cent. These increases are largely the result of increased immigration. The image of European countries with relatively homogeneous populations is increasingly outdated (OECD, 2000).

In addition to new arrivals, there are students who belong to groups who are either indigenous to the area or have lived in the country for several generations and whose home language is not that spoken in the school (defined here as 'bilingual learners'). Most European countries include at least one permanent group speaking a language different from the majority language. In France, for example, there are groups who speak Basque, Breton, Catalan, Corsican, Flemish, and a dialect of German.

In many Western European countries schools and colleges are under increasing pressure to find strategies to address the special needs of students whose home language is not the language used in school. These strategies have been influenced by the national and local sentiment regarding culture and language, attitudes toward immigration, and the available education resources. All further education colleges and adult learning centres will provide additional support in language skills to enable those whose language competence has the potential to limit their educational progress. Such support will be located under the banner of ESOL (English for Speakers of Other Languages).

Source: CHANGE Picture Bank. Used with permission

● **As soon as they learn Catalan, will they learn mathematics?**

Research carried out by Professor Núria Gorgorió working in Barcelona with new arrival children from Ecuador, Morocco and Pakistan has identified the importance of a shared language for communicating, specifically for the learning of mathematical concepts and skills. In addition, her work has shown that differences in number acquisition between varying cultural groups run deep, with cultural difference impacting on students' perceptions of how to approach number tasks.

Learners taking part in the research from a variety of cultural backgrounds expressed very differing cultural expectations of maths learning. Asian learners, for example, found the free-flowing discovery approach used in the Catalan classroom disruptive and operating against their learning needs. Chinese students, in particular, asked why the staff allowed so much noise in the classroom. A student from Pakistan could not understand why he was not beaten when he did not complete his homework. For learners there is a clear expectation of a 'norm' in the maths classroom, which in their minds and expectations affects Mathematics learning outcomes.

In focusing on teaching strategies the research revealed the varying approaches used in different countries to solving mathematical problems, with, for example, activities such as long division taught in different ways all over the world. The research revealed that teachers expect students to be number competent when using their preferred method, having the view that numbers have a universality not found in language. This approach was resulting in dire consequences for some students. The research revealed that when learners experience difficulties, the assumption is often that the student is at fault rather than the teacher or the teaching approaches being adopted. Students from Ecuador and Africa are reportedly told that their approach to number is flawed, while the European model is the 'correct' one (Gorgorió and de Abreau, 2009). Students using non-Western methods had their work downgraded and consequently developed negative feelings about their numeracy abilities.

Task 3.7

Review the Maths texts in common usage in an educational institution (possibly your workplace or training placement). Grade them from 1 (good) to 5 (poor) in terms of their language accessibility for different learner groups. Do they offer a range of methods as acceptable for number computation (as we do in this text) or does the text offer a 'one way only' approach?

The impact of poor skill levels

Government data illustrate the impact of poor number and literacy skills for men and women.

Figure 3.3 shows the standard percentage increase in wages earned by men and women over and above the non-qualified population who have literacy and numeracy Level 2 qualifications. Leitch records that improved basic skills moved 185,000 people into work between 1994 and 2004. In addition, employability at age 35 was strongly linked to having achieved basic skills in numeracy and literacy (Leitch Report, 2006).

Research carried out by PricewaterhouseCooper on the economic return on HE qualifications demonstrates the financial return on numeracy qualification, indicating that those with A level in Maths are likely to earn up to 10 per cent more by the age of 25 than those without. Learners who miss out in gaining numeracy qualifications

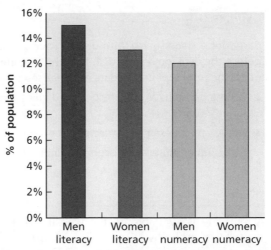

Figure 3.3 Increased earning potential (shown as a percentage) for those with qualifications above level 2 in numeracy and literacy

Source: Data collected from Department for Innovation, Universities and Skills (DIUS), Workforce Reform (2007)

when at school take a long time (if ever) to recover from their disadvantaged situation. It was research like this which led to the introduction of initiatives such as the Skills for Life programmes (Jenkins et al., 2007). In addition, research has defined a deficit in the UK's skills as highlighted in 'The Skills for Life' strategy introduced in March 2001, which was formulated as a response to 'A Fresh Start', the report produced by Claus Moser.

The Moser Report concluded that up to 7 million adults (one in five of the adult population in England) had difficulties with literacy and numeracy – a higher proportion than any other European country apart from Poland and Ireland. The aim of the Skills for Life strategy then is to ultimately eliminate the problem of poor levels of adult literacy and numeracy (National Audit Office, 2004:20).

The question of the classification of your level of skill is an interesting one. Some of the learners recorded as having number difficulties might be new arrivals keen to pass our numeracy tests in order to increase their chances of employment. Jenny's class described below provides an exemplification of this phenomenon.

Case study

Jenny, also a retired primary teacher (just like Liz in Chapter 1), is teaching numeracy in an inner London borough. Her class consists solely of Asian women, all with young children, who want to gain a qualification in number and in order to take up employment when their children are older. She finds her class very rewarding to teach but also demanding. Jenny reports:

'These are competent and capable students who want to pass a numeracy exam in a quick time scale. Sometimes they have finished the work I have prepared in double quick time and I have to think of some numeracy games and activities to keep them occupied. No matter how much work I throw at them, they rise to the challenge and complete it all.'

Task 3.8

Carry out a small survey with one of your groups of learners asking them how competent they are (on a scale of 1–5) with using literacy and numeracy. Ask the group to guess the results when the data are analysed for men and women separately.

● Do the group have any preconceived ideas about the numeracy skills of any particular ethnic groups?

● Are Asians, for example, expected to be better at number than their white counterparts?
Review the results and discuss the findings.

A template is available on the website for this book to help you with this task. Available from **www.pearsoned.co.uk/qtls**.

Number workout

Complete the exercises below. See if you improve in speed and accuracy by the time you reach the end of the book.

3.1 Number square – Sudoku
Place a number in each empty square so that every row and every column contains each of the numbers from 1 to 4.

	4	1	
1			2
4			1
	1	2	

3.2 The magic number

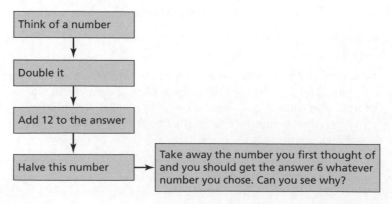

Think of a number

Double it

Add 12 to the answer

Halve this number → Take away the number you first thought of and you should get the answer 6 whatever number you chose. Can you see why?

3.3 Add up

If the number in each circle is the sum of the two below it, can you work out the top number?

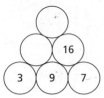

3.4 What is the smallest whole number with three digits?

Can you name this number?

1,000,000,000

3.5

a. 4 × 5 × 3
b. (harder) 7 × 9 × 4

Record in your portfolio how long it took you to complete this exercise.

- Did you need to use a calculator or were you able to complete all three sums in your head?
- What number strategies did you adopt to help you to succeed?

Summary

By the end of this chapter you should have:

- A better understanding of a range of barriers that impact on student learning.
- Begun to analyse tables and data and explored their meaning.
- Started to explore the significance of language as a support for number learning.

Reflections on Chapter 3

- What have you gained from reading this chapter?
- Are you more aware now of some of the issues involved with teaching number?
- Do you have any innovative ideas for exercises to use with your learners to make number fun? If so, record them in your ILP.

Part 2   TOOLS OF THE TRADE

In this part we refocus our attention on two key elements:

1 The curriculum requirements that are giving number work much more focus in all areas of the curriculum.
2 Your personal skill development as a teacher.

Together we will think about your competence with number and demonstrate practical ways in which you can plan for number activities in your teaching. In this section we offer a number of tools to help you and your learners develop their skills and record their achievements.

In the last chapter of this section we offer exemplar teaching material designed to support current approaches to teaching numeracy. In addition, we include some exemplar questions, similar to those designed by the Exam Boards, specifically for numeracy qualifications. Many of the examples used here are based on the types of questions that will be included in the numeracy tests for the functional skills qualifications (see Chapter 5). They are different from the questions previously offered as part of the Key Skills Award and, in our opinion, require more developed numeracy skills.

4 Numeracy in the curriculum

This chapter explores the FE curriculum from a number of perspectives and looks at a variety of models that have been used over time to raise numeracy standards. It explores early attempts to embed numeracy into every qualification at every level and introduces the reader to the focus given to numeracy as an applied subject in the new curriculum for 14–19 educations.

By the end of this chapter you will be able to:

- Discuss programmes of learning and qualifications available in schools and colleges.
- Understand how learners' achievement in Maths and numeracy might influence curriculum planning in your subject area.

In this chapter we explore changing curricular approaches to teaching numeracy.

The standards from the agreed competencies required of those training to teach in the Learning and Skills sector addressed in this chapter are:
AS 2, BS 1, BS 2, BS 3, DS1-3

This chapter relates to the following minimum core standards for numeracy:
A2 Develop personal numeracy knowledge and reflect upon own experiences

To set the scene this chapter starts with a task.

Task 4.1

Discuss with a peer your route into teacher training.

- How significant has the ability to achieve qualifications in numeracy been to your success?
- Can you name other careers where qualifications in number are seen as essential?
- Can you name any roles/occupations where number is not significant?

In order to offer a thorough analysis of the curriculum you will see described below the complex landscape (soon to be simplified) of qualifications currently available to learners. In providing this information our intention is that you should be as well prepared as possible for the qualifications you may have to work with during your teaching career.

Entry-level qualifications

These are in the form of certificates that can be taken in over 200 subjects, including basic skills qualifications in Numeracy, Literacy and ICT. These qualifications are specifically aimed at the following types of learner:

- students with learning difficulties and disabilities;
- those for whom English is a second language;
- those who may have been out of education for some time.

These qualifications have been designed and targeted at reducing the number of NEET (not in education, employment or training) in society and focusing on skills for employability and personal fulfilment.

GCSEs

GCSEs (General Certificates in Secondary Education) including vocational GCSEs currently coexist with new diploma lines of learning which are being gradually introduced into the school and college curriculum. The Diploma cannot be achieved without demonstration of numeracy skills. For a GCSE equivalent qualification, this will be at Level 2 in the New Qualification Framework (NQF) (see **www.qdca.org.uk**).

GNVQs

The future of vocational qualifications such as GNVQs (General National Vocational Qualifications) is currently unclear following the publication of the Wolfe Report in 2011. It is likely that new vocational qualifications will be introduced alongside focus on an English Baccalaureate.

● NVQs

NVQs (National Vocational Qualifications) are available in over 700 different subjects: construction, hairdressing, business, aromatherapy, management, administration, plumbing, and so on. Here again, the aim is to simplify the offer and reduce the complexity of the qualification landscape over the next few years.

● Key skills

Key skills can be studied in six areas and studied as a qualification in their own right. Numeracy is one of the six Key Skills. Demonstration of Key Skill competence forms an integrated part of all vocational (GNVQs and NVQs) qualifications and is assessed as an integral part of the core curriculum (as part of an A-level syllabus, for example).

● A levels

A levels (General Certificate of Education – Advanced Level) consist of two levels: AS (the first half of an A level as a self-standing qualification), and A2 level (the complete qualification). Under the current approach to curriculum reform (DfES, 2005) these qualifications remain, but with a reduced number of assessment points (from six down to four). In addition these qualifications may be disaggregated into two separate awards. The return of one final examination has also been intimated.

● AEAs

AEAs (Advanced Extension Awards) have been introduced to stretch talented A-level students. The aim is to allow able students to demonstrate their skills and aptitude more fully, with opportunities available for them to complete modules of university work at an early age.

● VCEs

Vocational Certificates in Education (VCEs, also known as vocational A levels) are available in a range of subjects, such as business and leisure and tourism, as progression from vocational GCSEs. Given the title 'applied A level', these qualifications, launched in summer 2005, have replaced advanced vocational provision, the intention being that employers and higher education institutions will accord the applied A level the same respect as given to A-level qualifications.

● PELTS

The Qualifications and Curriculum Development Authority (QCDA) has developed a draft single framework for personal, employment, learning and thinking skills (PELTS) for all learners aged 11 to 19. This framework combines the study of functional English, Mathematics and ICT, and is designed to equip young people with the skills they need to be employable and to achieve success in life.

Task 4.2

Record in your ILP your involvement with the qualification routes set out above.

- Have you been delivering the core curriculum in these areas?
- Has numeracy competence been developed separately or as an integrated part of the curriculum?
- If you have not been responsible for delivery components of number as part of your teaching portfolio, then who has been responsible and what approaches have they been taking to meet the curriculum requirements for the qualifications?

Clarify responsibilities for numeracy teaching and testing in relation to the courses you teach.

- Are you working collaboratively with all staff working on the same courses as you?
- What forms are those collaborations taking?

Having summarised the range of qualifications available, we move now to focus on the current reform under way which is intended, over the next few years, to have a major impact on the complex qualification landscape described above.

Task 4.3

Discuss with others in your team and debate the following question:

'The qualification landscape is too confusing and confused for learners. This is impacting on the opportunity afforded to them to such an extent that the post-14 curriculum is currently failing more than 50 per cent of the population it was designed to serve.'

Record your discussion and conclusions in your ILP.

14–19 curriculum reform

At the time of writing this text, major reform of the secondary and post-16 curriculum is under way. There is some ambiguity around the introduction of new qualifications known as 'Diplomas'. A phased introduction over a five-year period from 2008 until 2013 is planned. Integral to diploma achievement will be the demonstration of competence in functional skills: namely, Numeracy, Literacy and ICT. As a response to the ambiguity around Diploma introduction we offer below a series of questions (with answers) commonly asked about the new qualifications. Attention has been given to the elements of the proposed reform which will impact specifically on the skills curriculum (Numeracy, Literacy and ICT). Diploma take up rates have not been extensive. The future for some diploma qualifications looks bleak and the new coalition government explores the potential of baccalaureate type qualifications.

● What is the Diploma?

The Diploma is a new qualification for 14- to 19-year-olds that combines theoretical study with practical activities and develops skills that are highly valued by employers and universities. The Diploma gives students an insight into work and will help them make decisions about their future direction. The Diploma will provide the skills and knowledge needed for progression into employment and into further and higher education. The ability to use number in work-related settings will be a key focus in the Diploma. However, at the time of writing the last three planned lines of diploma learning in the more traditional areas of academic study – namely foreign languages, science and engineering – have been abolished and the future for diplomas is a little uncertain.

Why was the Diploma being introduced?

The Diploma is part of a bigger set of changes to education between the ages of 14 and 19 intended to ensure that all young people can choose a qualification that best suits their interests and learning style. GCSEs and A levels are also being updated, the number of Apprenticeships is being increased to 500,000 and the age to which young people will continue in education or training will be increased to 18. The DfES in 2009 expressed the view that the current options available at age 14 are not attractive to some students. Choice is limited, especially for those who prefer a more applied learning style, while today's vocational qualifications are sometimes not well understood or respected.

In addition, employers and universities report that those who pass through the current general qualifications route are not always able to express themselves effectively or perform basic calculations confidently. The ability to manage tasks productively without supervision is often lacking. Also, with higher than ever numbers achieving three grade As at A level, identifying the most able candidates is increasingly difficult.

It is intended that by creating a qualification that engages young people, and carries weight with employers and higher education – while promoting the skills crucial for success in both the modern workplace and university – the introduction of Diplomas should establish a dynamic response to government concerns. However, again, at the time of writing the future of some of the proposed Diploma lines of learning is looking a little bleak as a new government places its stamp on education policy.

Who has designed the Diploma?

Employers and universities have been integral to the creation of the Diploma. They have worked with representatives from schools, colleges and awarding bodies to set out what students with a Diploma need to have learnt. The involvement of employers in the design of the Diploma has led to a strong focus on numeracy skills.

What about other qualifications?

Other qualifications such as GCSEs, A levels and BTECs can be taken as part of a Diploma or as separate subjects alongside it. A levels and GCSEs will continue to be offered until at least the next major review in 2013. Other established qualifications such as BTECs and NVQs will continue to be available in their own right but will also be components of the Diploma. As take-up of the Diploma grows and the national entitlement is introduced in 2013, the government does not expect other qualifications to be available to young people unless they feature in the three main learning pathways: the Diploma, Apprenticeships and general qualifications.

● Will the Diploma be replacing any existing qualifications?

Diplomas will give young people new options alongside other qualifications like GCSEs, A levels and Apprenticeships. The Diploma will not replace existing qualifications. Many existing qualifications may be followed as part of additional or specialist learning, and contribute to a Diploma qualification.

It will be up to young people, parents, schools and colleges to decide whether the new Diplomas will offer them the best route to success. Because GCSEs and A levels are long-established and valued qualifications, their future will not be decided by a pre-emptive government decision, but instead by the demands of young people and schools.

The 14–19 White Paper sets out three main options for learning routes which young people can choose at different times: GCSEs and A levels, the applied work-related Diplomas, and work-based Apprenticeships.

● What are functional skills, and how do they fit with Diplomas?

Functional skills are the practical English, Maths and IT skills that everybody needs to deal with everyday life: for example, writing a letter of application, or working out the value of a car.

The Diploma will contain all three functional skills qualifications. This will ensure that young people secure the right foundation of English, Maths and ICT skills needed for progression into employment, college and university. Passes in functional skills will be required at level 1 for a Level 1 Diploma and at level 2 for a Level 2 or a Level 3 Diploma.

● What is a Diploma worth in the School and College Achievement and Attainment Tables?

The Diploma is available at three levels:

- *Foundation* – equivalent to 5 GCSEs at grades D to G.
- *Higher* – equivalent to 7 GCSEs at grades A* to C.
- *Advanced* – equivalent to 3.5 A levels.

A new Extended Diploma, designed to extend each of the 17 Diplomas by adding more generic and additional and specialist learning, will also be available from 2011.

The Extended Diplomas are expected to be equivalent to:

- *Foundation* – 7 GCSEs at grades D to G.
- *Higher* – 9 GCSEs at grades A* to C.
- *Advanced* – 4.5 A levels.

A summary of Diploma achievement and attainment (AAT) points is available on the QCDA website.

Full details of UCAS tariff points for the Diploma are available on the UCAS website.

Task 4.4

Explore one of the dimensions of the curriculum for which you have a responsibility and complete the table below. Identify the timescale for the 14–19 reform agenda impacting on your subject area. An example is provided to demonstrate the type of response you might make.

Name of course	Intended qualification	Rationale	Impact of the reform
Hospitality and Catering	GNVQ 3	To support the local hotel industry by providing qualified staff	Qualification to be replaced in 2009
			Redesign of content influenced by industry requirements
			Integration of functional skills as part of the core

Task 4.5

Consider how the qualification reforms will impact on your teaching role. Explore the focus of the proposals, the target group under consideration and the possible key motivators for the proposed change. In addition, consider what impact this policy will have on you and your role in your organisation.

Numeracy in the curriculum

At any time in the daily life of a teacher there is the potential for you to be asked to teach new areas of knowledge and new curricula. It is likely, for example, that you may be asked to support curriculum delivery of the new Diploma lines of learning. Before agreeing to increase your workload you may wish to consider the following questions, the responses to which may impact on your decision. The questions have been designed to encourage open engagement with your manager when asked to take on new areas of work. They have been designed to encourage an open dialogue, to help you seek clarification in order to accept the challenges and opportunities that have been put before you.

Q.1 How do you feel my expertise matches the curriculum areas you wish me to teach?

Q.2 What training is available to support me so that I can ensure I provide my learners with every opportunity to succeed?

If the request relates to a diploma qualification:

Q.3 How will the numeracy requirements for the programme be delivered? Is there an expectation that they will taught in a integrated manner as part of the core curriculum or will additional numeracy support be provided?

And some potential responses to Question 3:

- In some cases organisations are choosing to offer separate sessions to help learners achieve the numeracy skills for the Diplomas and to pass the numeracy tests. This model is currently used to support achievement of the GNVQ and other vocational routes which require demonstration of number competence.

- However, there is, in the spirit of the new Diploma design, an expectation that numeracy and literacy competence will be fully integrated into the specified line of learning. This is being advocated in an attempt to ensure that learners are numeracy and literacy competent in the context of their selected area of study. This is why it is important for you, when agreeing to take on new areas of teaching, to be clear about programme-delivery structures.

In answer to Question 2, there are a number of training programmes available free of charge to organisations delivering functional skills courses as part of the new Diploma qualification. Log on to **www.fssp.qia.org.uk**.

Number workout

Time yourself if you want to know whether you improve in speed as well as accuracy by the time you reach the end of the book. Questions become more difficult as you progress through the exercise.

4.1	**4.2**	**4.3**
a. $56 \div 8$	a. $5656 \div 8$	a. $153250 \div 5$
b. $108 \div 12$	b. $3926 \div 13$	b. $31815 \div 15$
c. $1005 \div 5$	c. $1566 \div 6$	c. $6544 \div 8$

Record in your portfolio how long it took you to complete this exercise. Did you need to use a calculator or were you able to complete all three sums in your head? What number strategies did you adopt to help you to succeed?

Summary

By the end of this chapter you should have:

- A better understanding of the focus on number that is impacting on all areas of the curriculum.
- Been made aware of the role number ability can play in all areas of life.

Reflections on Chapter 4

- What have you gained from reading this chapter?
- Are you more aware now of some of the issues involved with teaching number?
- Do you have any innovative ideas for exercises to use with your learners to make number fun? If so, record them in your ILP.

5 You and your learners

This chapter explores the level of qualification and competence in number expected of those teaching in the Learning and Skills sector. In addition it offers advice on planning matters associated with the introduction of number activities using both schemes of work and lesson plans.

The standards from the agreed competencies required of those training to teach in the Learning and Skills sector addressed in this chapter are:

AS 3, BS 1, CS1, CS2, CS3, DS1-3

This chapter relates to the following minimum core standards for numeracy:

A 2 The extent of the knowledge, understanding and number skills expected of all teachers in the Learning and Skills sector

A 2 Awareness of methods and purpose, using strategies to make sense of a situation using number

---

KEY WORDS   **legislative requirements**   **level descriptors**   **Individual Learning Plans**

The context

Government focus on the ability and skills of the UK population in relation to number, particularly in respect to its use and application to the world of work, has been considerable. The outcome of this interest (discussed in Part 1 of this text) has impacted on the training of those preparing to work, and already qualified to teach in the Learning and Skills sector. There is a clear focus on teaching how to teach numeracy embedded into all programmes of training in the sector.

Requirements for staff

There is an expectation that staff teaching in the sector will be competent in working with the Key Skills at Level 2 as a minimum. Within the new qualification structure for lecturers in the sector, opportunities are available for training and development to support those needing to address different curricular requirements at different times in their careers.

If you are studying for the initial award as part of the first stage to becoming a fully qualified teacher for the LSS, you are expected to be able to function at least at Level 2 in all the Key Skills areas (including Numeracy). To gain full qualification status QTLS, lecturers are required to demonstrate competence in all three Key Skill areas (Numeracy, Literacy and ICT) at Level 2. The Level 2 descriptor is shown in Table 5.1.

> The Adult Numeracy Core Curriculum can be accessed at the following website: **www.excellencegateway.org.uk/sflcurriculum**.

Working with your learners

Government expectations are that those training to teach in the Learning and Skills sector know how to encourage their learners to use number with confidence. This focus on numeracy is not just located around how to teach number, but has a wider scope. New curricular requirements have made it compulsory for trainee teachers themselves to understand the number skills required in the world of work. Teachers will need to understand and work with the requirements of number in a range of vocational and work contexts. Here in Part 2 we offer practical support and strategies to increase learner engagement.

Table 5.1 Level descriptors for the Key Skills award

Framework level	Level indicators
Level 2	Level 2 qualifications recognise the ability to gain a good knowledge and understanding of a subject area of work or study, and to perform varied tasks with some guidance or supervision. Learning at this level involves building knowledge and/or skills in relation to an area of work or a subject area and is appropriate for many job roles

Using ILPs to develop your skills and those of your learners

Chapter 1 introduced you to an Individual Learning Plan tool (ILP). You were asked to evaluate your personal numeracy skills and produce an action plan to address any areas where potential weaknesses might lie.

Task 5.1

Return to the ILP you completed in Chapter 1 and consider the following:

- Did completion of the ILP identify any issues for you?
- Did it motivate you to take further action in respect of your personal number skills?
- Do you feel the ILP process is productive and could it help your learners?

The use of ILPs extends beyond that suggested here in this text with ILPs being used by all LSS learners as a key part of their course. It is through the ILP process that achievements towards qualification requirements can be monitored appropriately. This focus on the individual learner and their needs means that the lecturer working in the LSS will need to be mindful of the National Curriculum frameworks, will be required to understand the basic skills needs of specific students and be able to provide extension opportunities for the talented student in the vocational and/or academic context. The focus on what are known as *key skills* – namely numeracy, literacy, ICT (the hard skills) – and the soft skills of problem solving, working with others and improving own learning and performance, is also increased. As more Diploma lines of learning are introduced in both schools and colleges as part of the 14–19 reform agenda, the focus on numeracy will remain described in the terminology of 'functional' rather than 'key' skills.

Learner assessment

It is a requirement that all learners in full-time education, and those enrolled on National Employer Training Programmes (NETPs) and registered with an education provider, receive an initial assessment of their functional skills in the subjects of Numeracy, Literacy and ICT. A number of bespoke tools are available to identify the individual's operational level in key areas and highlight whether they will need additional support to be able to continue with their programme of study.

All learners have an entitlement to free additional support in the functional skill areas should the assessment show that they are operating below the standard needed for the course of study they are deemed able to follow.

Sometimes additional support will be provided for whole-class groups; on other occasions it will be offered on a one-to-one basis. The information from the initial assessment, together with reports from previous institutions, academic results achieved, and the record made at the point the learner applied for the course and was interviewed all form part of the Individual Learning Plan.

The practical use of Individual Learning Plans

Individual Learning Plans are used by teachers, personal tutors and students themselves to design a programme of study and to track its progress. In the college environment, and one would hope elsewhere in the sector, it is considered appropriate that all learners should be entitled to a negotiated and agreed programme of study. This should be planned with their personal tutor or teacher, taking their individual needs into account. Progress in relation to the ILP needs to be reviewed regularly.

The standard 'model' ILP combines a number of functions: planning the student's programme, keeping a student record and monitoring the student's progress. For most students, the ILP brings together various documents that are used at different stages of their programme. The ILP provides the tutor with a guide to what work needs to be covered with the student, and a structured record in which to log outcomes and actions. The nature and complexity of the ILP will vary according to the duration of the programme, whether full time, part time over 180 hours, short part time, or work based.

The ILP model used in your college or institution will probably be available on the corporate intranet. The format may be varied according to the needs of the individual programme. However, the overall structure and the ground covered usually remain consistent. Examples of *ILPs for your learners* can be downloaded from the companion website (www.pearsoned.co.uk/qtls).

ILPs normally cover:

● Student record (full time/part time);

● Key/functional skill planning and tracking;

● Initial assessment and study support planning;

● Proformas for student self-assessment and one-to-one tutorial interviews;

● Tutor log to record discussions and reviews against the set targets.

Working with a group of learners

If appointed as a course tutor, you will be required to keep up-to-date information on the learning needs of all your tutees. Part of this information should be a record of initial diagnostic test results completed by each student. During each ILP interview the progress of your tutees should be checked to ensure they are persevering with the achievement of the basic and key skills required to complete their qualification. Table 5.2 is a tutor's record of a group of learners who have numeracy needs. These learners are the group identified as level2 @ 19, targeted in the 14–19 reform agenda (DfES, 2005) as typical underachievers who need support to develop and progress in the core skills. The three columns headed 'initial assessment', 'diagnostic result' and 'free writing score' identify the three diagnostic tools used in the institution. (Learner names are fictitious.)

Table 5.2 Tutor record for a group with numeracy needs

Name	First name	DoB	Student no	Date	Subject	GCSE Maths	Initial assessment	Diagnostic result for Level 1 Assessment	Free writing score	Identified needs	Current status	Type of support
Allen	Ewan	15/10/89	007630	6/9/07	Numeracy	D	L1	76%	11		OK	
Brown	Chris	22/06/90	007549	6/9/07	Numeracy	D	L1	62%	12		Withdrawn	
Brown	Mat	18/04/90	007657	6/9/07	Numeracy	E	L1	87%	13	Hearing loss	Support	In class
Crisps	Simon	20/04/90	007541	6/9/07	Numeracy	F	E3	72%	10			
Fletcher	Lucy	3/12/89	007292	15/9/07	Numeracy	U	Absent	Absent	10			
Elan	Narjit	12/4/90	007293	6/9/07	Numeracy	U	E3	20%	5	Additional support		1-to-1
Taylor	Emma	21/3/90	007294	6/9/07	Numeracy	D	L1	79%	13		Support	In class
Moore	Mary	3/10/89	007300	6/9/07	Numeracy	E	L1	87%	13		Support	In class
Radshaw	Carl	20/10/89	007298	6/9/07	Numeracy					ESOL	Support	

L = Level of Assessment Test

E = English as a Second Language

Source: Adapted from a form used in a college of further education

5

51

Task 5.2

Review Table 5.1.

● What does this information tell you about this group of learners?

● If you were the tutor for this particular group, what actions would you instigate as a result of receiving this information?

Task 5.3

Look again at Table 5.1, specifically at Narjit who is a second-language English user. His numeracy score is much lower than that for other members of your class.

● What advice can you offer Narjit?

● Other than talking to Narjit, what options are available to you?

Explore the additional support available in your organisation for learners whose competence in the core skills is limiting their ability to achieve.

Planning to meet individual needs

Once in possession of information about your learners, it is your responsibility to use this information effectively to help learners stay on track. Whether you are a trainee teacher on placement or one already employed and developing your skills 'on the job', any experience you can get working directly with individual learners is worthwhile. Once you take on full responsibilities as a course tutor, you will be required to keep a record of your learners' progress and to monitor this throughout their time with you. Regular meetings with learners need to be planned into any tutorial scheme of work.

At these meetings you will keep a record of the learners' progress and development, highlighting any areas or problems and acknowledging their successes. This is also the point at which you set targets and motivate learners to reach the end of their training. Such targets will be recorded on an Individual Learning Plan (ILP) similar to the one you may be completing as part of your record of the tasks set in this book. The ILP should belong to the learner but, as a course tutor, you should keep an independent record. This should inform your planning when considering both your schemes of work and your lesson plans.

● Supporting specific needs through appropriate planning

Assuming you are the tutor for the group of students listed in Table 5.2, you may wish to work with them during tutorial sessions to support them in the development of their numeracy skill and confidence. Number games, for example, might become a regular start to every day, attendance data could be interrogated and classroom design explored.

It is not usual to plan tutorial sessions in any detail. However, there is an expectation that core lessons will be. Below is an example of a Key Skills Numeracy Lesson Plan designed by a lecturer responsible for teaching Health and Social Care.

Table 5.3 Lesson plan

Name of lecturer: **Fred**	Course: **Health and Social Care: Intermediate (GCSE) Vocational Qualification: numeracy key skills**
Room: **A21**	Session: **Friday session 4**
Start time: **3.30pm**	Finish time: **4.30pm**
Number of participants: **15**	Significant issues: **This is not a good time for the topic. Attendance will need monitoring and activities designed to ensure student enthusiasm is achieved and maintained**
Aims	**To develop students' ability to estimate in varying contexts using appropriate measuring tools**
Objectives	By the end of the session participants will be able to: ● **Use and evaluate two different systems of measurement** ● **Recognise and apply two different measuring systems to different dimensions of estimation** ● **Recognise the significance of error in estimation**

Time	*Lesson content*	*Method*	*Resources*
3.30 5 minutes	Settle group and clarify objectives Emphasise how functional the session will be in supporting key skill achievements	Link to key skill competence and illustrate how functional the session will be in supporting participants in achieving the skill	Key skills record book for each student Objectives identified on the board
10 minutes	Allocate groups Distribute local maps	Mixed ability groupings	Maps
	Set tasks: Identify location of all the nurseries in the region	Small-group activity	Record sheet for estimations
	Estimate the walking distance between each one	Worksheet identifying names of each nursery	Record outcomes
5 minutes	Compare outcomes	Large-group brainstorm	Board work
3 minutes	Record agreed estimated distances (metres), in walking time (minutes) and car transport (minutes)	Gapped handout	Paperwork available
10 minutes	Using a stopwatch, send two (trustworthy) students to the on-site nursery and record how long it takes them to return On return, compare actual time taken with the estimated time	Remaining students to discuss how long it takes them to travel to their work placements and explore the implications of their method of transport	Stopwatch Discussion sheet
5 minutes	Record outcome of the discussion	Students to compare journey times, external influences that impact on their travel plans	Chart to complete which compares journey times with travel method

(continued)

Table 5.3 Lesson plan (continued)

Time	Lesson content	Method	Resources
5 minutes	Explore the impact of esti-mated time of journey being much less than actual	Discussion linked to their professional responsibili-ties as carers	Key questions provided to direct discussion
5 minutes	Collate ideas	Brainstorm and record	Board or flipchart
5 minutes	Individuals to draw up a code for travel when on work placement	Gapped handout	Worksheet provided
7 minutes	Conclusions, revision of activity, key learning points	Return to the objectives	Record achieve-ment, if appropri-ate, in the individu-al student key skills record book

Notice times, content, method and resources. For those who like making lists of things to do, your lesson plan will come as a useful tool; others may need to make more effort to commit to writing. The value of such plans cannot be overestimated, and there is certainly an expectation with the LSS (monitored through external inspection) that staff will plan the periods of formal activity they engage in with learners.

Task 5.4

Consider how you might develop some of the number skills used in this session.

- How will you consolidate the learning that has taken place?
- What will you focus on, next time you meet this group of learners?

A template for this lesson plan can be downloaded from the companion website **www.pearsoned.co.uk/qtls**.

Schemes of work and course aims

Schemes of work

Schemes of work might best be described as the *grand design* for a set period (term, year, semester). They could be compared with a holiday itinerary in which you plan where you are going to visit in general terms, perhaps with the intention of visiting cer-tain sites, but do not at this stage identify exactly what you will do on each day of your holiday. Reece and Walker (1999: 315) describe a scheme of work as 'a series of planned learning experiences, sequenced to achieve the course aims in the most effective way'.

Schemes of work are long- or medium-term plans designed to ensure progression and continuity in learning over a period of time. They should be 'a working document which summarises teachers' thinking about a course, providing a structure and offer-ing guidelines for more detailed lesson planning' (Balderstone and Lambert, 2000: 69).

● Course aims

The starting point in the design of any scheme of work is the course aims. What is the overarching purpose of this course, what areas of the curriculum are relevant and what skills do I want the participants to achieve?

Increasingly, course aims are determined by the external organisations that award the qualification. In many subjects the curriculum is divided into units of study, with the aims of each unit specified in advance. You will need to ensure your scheme of work matches the course content as set out by the approved syllabus for the programme. You may have some choice over the order in which you address the aims and the way in which you interpret the intended syllabus content, and this is where your experience and training are useful. It is important to plan carefully the order in which you frame each lesson in any time period.

The box below shows a list of questions to consider when presented with or designing course aims. The questions are designed to help you think about sequencing, planning for learning outcomes and student needs. In other words, using the holiday itinerary analogy, they are the practical questions you need to ask yourself before you set out on your journey.

5

Planning to achieve your aims

- What do I hope to achieve in the time available?
- What ideas, knowledge, skills and attitudes do I want to explore?
- What is going to be most helpful for this group of learners?
- What do I need to cover first before the learners can progress to more complex activities?
- Are there any sensitivities associated with the topic for those present? (These might relate to religious belief, ethnicity, health-related topics, political ideas.) If this is the case, consider how well you know the group, how long it might take to build up their confidence and trust before they might be able to tackle potentially sensitive issues.
- Should some material be presented in chronological order to support understanding?
- When can I hope that the group will be confident enough to engage with different teaching strategies such as role play and discussion, and which topics will be best covered using these strategies?
- Are there any safety issues I should address at the beginning of the course? (This might well apply in a workshop or practical situation.)
- Do I need access to any specific resources (when will the computer room or a guest speaker be available?), and how can I sequence the lessons that go before and come afterwards so that the most can be made of these opportunities?
- When will be best to assess learning?
- How, when and how often should I invite the learners to evaluate the learning experience?

Table 5.4 shows a scheme of work for an advanced leisure and tourism course on the topic of 'The holiday industry'. Notice how the lesson themes are ordered to support learner confidence and develop specific skills.

Table 5.4 Scheme of work for Advanced Vocational Qualification Leisure and Tourism

Topic: The holiday industry

Based on a timetable of two sessions per week, each of 90 minutes' duration

Key aim	Key knowledge	Key ideas	Skills	Resources	Assessment evidence	Aspects of performance
Week 1 ● Introduce the industry ● Ask why we study it ● What do we need to know?	Financial role of the holiday industry in the economies of some countries	For many countries the holiday industry is the mainstay of the economy. This has an impact on the country's approach to the customer	● Understanding of economic principles (numerical skills) ● Research skills in relation to country and economy ● Discussion skills (communication of experiences) ● Enquiry and questioning skills	● Maps ● Chalk and board ● Photographs ● Brochures ● ICT internet searches	● List of countries and economic stability ● Database of information ● Summary of discussion ● Key points identified	● Understanding of place and function ● Ability to relate knowledge and experience to demonstrate an understanding of impact
Week 2 ● Explore the countries which rely most heavily on the holiday industry and why	Specific countries and regions	The importance of the industry to the economy has an impact on client experience	● Identify regions and reasons ● Select one for study ● Work in a group ● Distribute tasks ● Work cooperatively with a team	● Internet access ● Worksheet ● Holiday brochures	● Comparison of brochure image of a selected region with that presented by internet research ● Tasks allocated for a group presentation	● Ability to work in a team ● Ability to use sources of evidence to present a viewpoint ● Understanding of place

56

Week	Learning objectives	Key questions	Skills	Resources	Assessment	Learning outcomes
Week 3	• Explore the region in detail in relation to quality of life for the inhabitants • Discuss impact of available resources on life experiences	• In what ways has the selected region used its resources to support the holiday industry? • What other industries entered or exited previously? • What impact do they have on the holiday industry?	• Research • Analysis • Enquiry and questioning skills • Extracting information from a video	• Internet access • Holiday brochures • Worksheet • Video section 'poor kids/rich kids'	• Research evidence • Analysis of video through a worksheet questionnaire	• Ability to use sources of evidence to present a viewpoint • Understanding of place • Ability to understand the impact of poverty on life chances
		• Key components of the holiday industry (what is on offer?) • What other industries survive or have declined in recent years? • Resources gained from the holiday industry have a key impact on life changes				
Week 4 Identify the implication of findings for the holiday Industry	• The impact of industrial decline • How can evidence of the past be used to enhance to experience of holidaymakers today?	• Helping the country visited to exploit its resources to the benefit of all • Enhancing the experience of the holiday-maker while providing support to the country	• Presentation skills • Numerical analysis • Teamwork • Independent learning • Ethical responsibility issues	• Group presentation requirements • Clear grading criteria previously discussed with the student group	Group presentation Individual report	• Ability to work as a team to present a thoroughly researched topic • Ability to think critically about the impact of the holiday industry on the selected region

5

Table 5.5   Scheme of work for basic skills in computing

Course title **Computers for beginners**	Qualification aim: **Basic skills Introduction equivalent to Learndirect 1st Certificate**		Start date **8 Nov.**	End date **13 Dec.**	Course code **Course leader**	**ICT/BA 1 To be confirmed**
Target enrolment number **15**	Attendance **15 Nov**	Attendance **29 Nov**	Number completing	Day of week: Monday Start **9.30** Finish **11 am**	Level **Basic skills 1, 2 and 3**	Venue **ICT room 104**

Week no. and date	*Session title*	*Content*	*Activities and skills*	*Assessment*	*Resources*
1 Monday, 8 Nov.	Introduction to computers	By the end of the session participants will: • be provided with details of the course • have received an introduction to the core computer concepts • understand turn on and log off facilities • have understood the importance of saving data	Individuals will learn through: • demonstration • activity • practice • following worksheet directions • self-practice and exploration	• Observation of basic skills • Gapped handout to confirm • Understanding of vocabulary	• Whiteboard • Handouts • A computer per participant • Worksheet
2 Monday, 15 Nov.	Consolidation of previous work	Brief test of language and function By the end of the session participants will: • have practised their typing skills • know how to save a document • have used the copy and paste function	Verbal non-threatening questioning • Teacher demonstration • Practice activities • Saving documents to disk	Test understanding and memory levels • Discussion • Brainstorm • Practice sheets • Handouts • Set homework	Quick test of last week's work • Whiteboard • Handouts • A computer per participant • Worksheet • Floppy disk per participant
3 Monday, 22 Nov.	Working together	Brief test of language and function By the end of the session participants will understand: • page set-up • margins • tables • how to design a template for a menu	Individuals learn through: • demonstration • activity • practice • following worksheet directions • self-practice and exploration • group work	Check progress with homework • Discussion • Brainstorm • Practice sheets • Handouts • Set homework	Quick test of last week's work • Whiteboard • Handouts • A computer per participant • Worksheet • Floppy disk per participant

Another example of a scheme of work, using a different template, is provided in Table 5.5. This scheme relates to a beginners' session in ICT skills.

A scheme of work template can be downloaded from the companion website **www.pearsoned.co.uk/qtls**.

The template used for the leisure and tourism session in Table 5.4 has some advantages over the ICT format as it allows space to record opportunities for achievement of certain skills. Where you are required to incorporate key skills into your curriculum, this design will be useful.

Task 5.5

Consider how numeracy skills might be incorporated into a scheme of work in your area. Think about how number work might play a key part of every session. What particular approaches will you adopt to encourage your learners to become more number competent?

Summary

In this chapter you will have:

- Reviewed your progress as a competent user of number by referring back to your number skills assessment and assessed your personal progress.
- Been introduced to the tools of teaching in the form of schemes of work and lesson plans in order that you might consider the integration of number work more closely into your planning.

Number workout

Time yourself if you want to know whether you improve in speed as well as accuracy by the time you reach the end of the book. Questions become more difficult as you progress through the exercise.

5.1
a. $56 \div 8 \times 7$
b. $108 \div 12 \times 11$
c. $155 \div 5 \times 7$

5.2
a. $56 \div 8 \times 13$
b. $390 \div 13 \times 21$
c. $1590 \div 5 \times 3$

5.3
a. $1566 \div 6 \times 9$
b. $6345 \div 15 \times 7$
c. $6664 \div 8 \times 9$

6 Some ideas and preparation for the tests

The ambition for every teacher/lecturer, whatever their subject, should be to produce learners who can identify problems and challenges and then find effective solutions. Within the area of numeracy it is important that learners can apply their knowledge to real-life work situations in order to become effective and competent employees. To this end it is essential that teachers help learners to become confident users of number by helping them to:

- recognise situations in which mathematics can be used;
- make sense of these situations;
- describe the situations using the correct mathematical terminology;
- analyse situations using number in order to inform judgements;
- interpret the mathematical outcomes in terms of the situation;
- communicate results and outcomes effectively.

In addition you will be encouraged to use strategies to promote and encourage communication of mathematical ideas both between teachers and learners and learners themselves.

The standards from the agreed competencies required of those training to teach in the Learning and Skills sector addressed in this chapter are:

AS 2, BS 1, BS 2, BS 3, DS1-3

This chapter relates to the following minimum core standards for numeracy:

A2 Develop personal numeracy knowledge and reflect upon own experiences

AS 1, AS4

KEY WORDS   vocational   active learning   problem-based learning

The learning theory which underpins our approach to teaching numeracy is that of situated learning. Throughout this text the ideas we have advocated underpin a situated approach, namely:

- that learning together can be more productive and effective than learning alone;
- that when learning takes on a purpose and relevance, more people are likely to benefit from it.

The situated learning approach has routes in the work of Lave.

Situated learning

Lave (1988) argues that learning as it normally occurs is a function of the activity, context and culture in which it takes place (i.e. it is situated). Social interaction is seen as a critical component of situated learning with learners becoming involved in a 'community of practice'. The approach acknowledges that new learners can benefit from the experienced, and that group learning can support the weaker students and enhance the confidence of the stronger.

Key principles of situated learning

1 Knowledge needs to be presented and learned in an authentic context: that is, settings and applications that would normally involve that knowledge.
2 Learning requires social interaction and collaboration.

As well as method and context, as highlighted above, there are other broadly described key skills required in the competent use of number. These are those of *representation* (making sense of situations), *analysis* (processing and using mathematics) and *interpretation* (understanding number in order to communicate results and inform decisions). The activity described below incorporates all three of these skills and can be adapted to a variety of vocational contexts in line with the theoretical approach adopted in situated learning theories.

● Representation

The exercises in Chapter 10 on Space and Shape, in Chapter 11 where graphs are used and in Chapter 9 on measurement all support the development of representation skills. The following activities might also be used.

Marketing your business (in any vocational context)

Working in groups, your learners are required to design a poster advertising their potential future workplace. The groups are encouraged to use numbers, diagrams, symbols, pictures, graphs and shapes but only five words. Once the task is completed, the group present their poster for judging by describing to the audience the design they have adopted. The criterion for success is the poster which presents the clearest and most informative picture using number in a creative way.

Such a task would help learners if asked any of the following questions in a functional skills test.

Potential question

Level 1

Sam is going to tile his bathroom. He will use black and white square tiles. Each tile in the section below is 6cm square. How many tiles will he need to order to cover an area 36cm by 36cm?

Sam decides to tile the area around the bath like this:

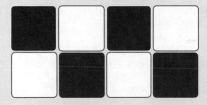

The wall is 2m long. He wants five rows of tiles above the bath.

● How many of each colour tile will Sam need to buy?
● If each tile costs £3.50 what will the bill be for tiling this wall?

The sample question could be adapted and, indeed, the level of challenge increased for learners operating with higher levels of numeracy competence.

● Analysis

Skills of analysis are addressed in Chapters 7, 8 and 11. The sort of activity you could use to develop these skills is as follows.

Dragons' Den

A version of this popular TV series can be played out in most learning contexts with vocational specialists asked to design a business plan for a new invention or venture. Costs and analysis of project outcomes will need to be presented to a chosen panel of judges.

Sequencing

Here your learners work in pairs or individually to solve a problem. This might be a mathematical calculation (cut into a series of steps) that needs to be reordered or a structure or a design that needs to be reassembled.

Making number come alive

Working in groups, give your learners a series of large cards with number notation on them. Give the group five minutes to create a mathematical sum which involves each group member with some responsibility for the sequence. After the allotted time ask the group to hold up their cards at the front of the group. This can lead on to debate and discussion in relation to other potential number sequences and results.

Planning an event

The exercise below, which could form part of the Adult Numeracy Level 1 curriculum activity, relates to planning an event. This could involve opening a new business venture, organising a party, or celebrating a business success. If your area is Childcare then adapt the activity for a children's party but do remove the alcohol!!

Party invitation

Draw a picture here.

Questions

The event starts at 6.30 p.m. and finishes at 8 p.m.

● How long does it last?

You need to book the venue.

● From what time will you book it?

If the cost is £15 per hour –

● How much will the venue cost?

You are providing food for 100 guests. The catering company will charge £10.00 per head.

● How much will the food cost?

Drinks

You decide to buy these yourself as the local supermarket will provide free glasses if you spend more than £50. The costs are as follows:

12 cans of beer £10.00

Wine is £3.20 per bottle

Lemonade is £1 per litre

● Produce an order for alcohol, spending no more than £70.

Disco

You are paying for a disco – the DJ wants a cheque for three hundred and forty pounds and six pence.

● How will you write that in numbers?

This example, again, is for Level 1 learners.

● Interpretation

The activities below represent ways in which skills of interpretation as covered in Chapters 7, 8, and 11 might be covered in a class situation. This highlights one of the advantages of teaching a vocation subject in the opportunity it affords you to plan large, innovative and creative projects. The example below offers endless possibilities for numeracy work. It can be adapted to fit a range of contexts.

Business Studies Activity

To plan the best location for a new branch of a supermarket chain

This task might be adapted to relate to a new nursery, sports centre, retail park, construction site and so on. The potential to incorporate a range of numeracy skills here is vast. Learners can work out journey times, access routes, material costs, build design, The activity could become a major piece of work lasting a number of weeks culminating in group presentations on preferred site, costs involved, and logistics involved in the proposal.

Definition Bingo

This is a good quick activity to revise a topic just covered, to check some basic understandings, as a novel way to set a test and as a lesson conclusion at the close of a session.

How to go about this task

● Ask the group to draw freehand a blank nine-square bingo grid.

● Write 12 mathematical terms or number answers on the board.

● Ask the group to write nine of these answers into their nine-square grid.

● Call 'Eyes down' and read out the definitions of the key words, or the number questions pulled at random from a bag.

● Learners then cross off the terms on their card if and when they match the definitions. When a line (horizontal, vertical or diagonal) is formed, they call 'Bingo!' and read back the key terms and their meaning.

Number Dominoes

Prepare a set of large cards each divided in half by a line similar to those used in a game of dominoes. Each contains a question and answer that do not match. The cards are then distributed around the class, one to each student. The game begins, and after much noise and movement (and fun) a sequence of domino-linked numbers and questions has been created.

Beat the Expert

Ask your learners to set you some number tasks for a change. Can you answer their questions in a set time?

Here is an exemplar question from a numeracy paper which requires skills of interpretation. This time at Level 2.

Question

Weight to Lose (WTL) is advertised as a new diet tablet to help people lose weight. A television programme wants to check whether this claim is correct. To find out, 44 males are selected and divided into groups A,B,C,D. They are weighed before and after the experiment. The results are shown in the experimental results tables.

Each group has a different exercise programme and diets:

- Group A = regular walking and a placebo* tablet
- Group B = regular walking, a calorie-controlled diet and WTL tablets
- Group C = workout five times a week, a calorie-controlled diet and placebo
- Group D = workout five times a week, a calorie-controlled diet and WTL tablets

The results are shown below.

Group A

Member	Age	Weight change (kg)
1	31	−1
2	25	−9
3	29	−5.5
4	24	−7.5
5	30	−2.5
6	32	+3
7	23	−1.5
8	27	−11.5
9	31	+4
10	26	+2
11	30	−0.5

Group B

Member	Age	Weight change (kg)
12	23	−2
13	28	+2
14	31	−6.5
15	24	−5
16	25	+0.5
17	30	−9
18	24	−5
19	30	−3.5
20	31	+2.5
21	27	−5.5
22	27	+2.5

*A placebo is a fake that has no active ingredients. Those taking the placebo will not be told this fact.

Group C

Member	Age	Weight change (kg)
23	28	−2.5
24	18	−1
25	30	−10
26	27	−8.5
27	23	−4.5
28	28	−3
29	27	−4
30	25	−7.5
31	31	−6.5
32	27	−9.5
33	31	−5

Group D

Member	Age	Weight change (kg)
34	28	−10
35	29	−11.5
36	30	0
37	32	−2.5
38	25	−11
39	25	−8.5
40	28	−0.5
41	31	−10.5
42	25	−1.5
43	27	0
44	30	−10

Learner task

Assuming all participants took the tablets and completed the exercise programme as directed, investigate the claim that the WTL diet tablets help people to lose weight.

You must show your calculations and state how you have used them to get your answer.

(N.B. A page of A4 blank paper is provided, plus another page for working out the calculations. 18 marks are available for this question.)

Learner assessment

The advantages of completing a large piece of work become apparent when you examine the guidance for a test question at Level 3, as offered below. The time allowed is 1 hour and 30 minutes.

Tutor guidance available for this task states:

● Learners are required to complete this assessment activity under supervised conditions.

● Learners are allowed to use calculators.

The following resources must be provided:

● Price information for each sport item.

● A diagram of the playing area (court, pitch, etc.).

Assessment task

In this assessment the learner is required to consider the costs involved in taking up a new sport. The learner is required to:

● Decide on the sport they wish to take up.

● Investigate what equipment they will need and decide upon six items they wish to buy.

- Find prices for all the items on their list from two different suppliers.
- Calculate the total costs from each supplier.
- Decide which items they will buy from which supplier and prepare a costing sheet.
- Assuming one supplier offers 10 per cent discount if all the purchases are made from him/her, calculate the best price available for the total spend and decide whether to accept the 10 per cent reduction.

Pitch activity

- Describe the shape of the pitch/court.
- Calculate the overall size.
- Imagine the court/pitch needs a new surface. Using the calculation of £23 for a grass surface and £45 for a hard surface, calculate the costs to resurface in both of these materials.
- Assuming the owner decides to grass the main part of the area up to 70 per cent of the surface, calculate the cost of using the hard material on the remaining surface. This task will require calculations to include assessment of the surface area. Draw a scale drawing to show where each section of material will be used.

It may not be possible to prepare your learners for every part of an assessment but as much practice as you can offer them will be extremely helpful.

Should you wish to access other test materials then log on to the websites for the examination awarding bodies and there you will be able to download previously used test papers.

The websites you need are: **www.edexcel.org.uk**, **www.ocr.org.uk**, **www.cityandguilds.org.uk**.

Summary

In this chapter you will have:

- Worked with number in a range of practical ways.
- Experienced the use of number work in everyday-life contexts.

Part 3   NUMBER COMPETENCE

In this part of the book we focus on deepening your understanding of number. The emphasis has shifted to support the development of your personal skills and to enhance your confidence to include aspects of numeracy in your teaching. To repeat our earlier claim, we feel that competence and confidence are inextricably linked. Working through the following chapters to master your own skills will enable you to teach numeracy more effectively: borrow some of the ideas and practices developed here to use in your teaching. Links to the Core Curriculum will be provided but it should be remembered that not everything in the Core will be covered in this text. The Excellence Gateway site, **www.excellencegateway.org.uk**, provides additional and comprehensive advice and support.

Each of the chapters in this section can be studied independently so that you can, if you wish, top up your skills in just one or two areas. Tasks at the end of each chapter are based on the topics covered within that particular chapter.

We suggest that you complete the **self-evaluation** and **target-setting grids**, examples of which are shown below. Chapter-specific versions appear at the end of each chapter and on the companion website at **www.pearsoned.co.uk/qtls**.

● Self-evaluation

Numeracy skill	*Personal competence*			*Confidence in providing opportunities for learners to use this skill*		
As covered within each chapter e.g. Percentages	High (H)	Medium (M)	Low (L)	H	M	L
Fractions	H	M	L	H	M	L

● Target setting

- Based on your self-evaluation, decide on appropriate target(s).
- Be realistic and set achievable but challenging targets.

Target(s)	Date for completion	Date achieved
e.g. Introduce the idea of estimation into my teaching sessions.		

7 Mental and written calculations

This chapter will encourage you to think about different types of numbers and the wide range of mental and written strategies which are available to you. It will not be an exhaustive list and it is likely that you know of other ways of performing the same or similar calculations. The approach here is to demonstrate a number of ways in which mental and written calculations might be undertaken, allowing you to select your preferred method.

By the end of this chapter you will understand:

- Number systems and patterns.
- The four operations: addition, subtraction, multiplication and division.
- Estimation.
- Different sorts of numbers including fractions.

> *The minimum core standards for numeracy referred to in this chapter are:*
> N1   L2.1   L2.2   L2.5   L2.6
> N2   L2.1   L2.2   L2.4   L2.5   L2.6

Number systems: an introduction

Learners of number today are encouraged to use whatever method they understand and can use efficiently. This may well differ from your personal experience of learning number. In the past learners were instructed to work in the way considered best or the one preferred by their teacher at that particular time. The commonly held view today is that if it works and is efficient, then, although other methods may be discussed, no particular approach is mandatory. With this in mind the chapters in Part 3 of this book offer opportunities to study approaches to numerical calculations which may differ from your own approach. This will help you to understand your students' methods more easily.

The techniques in this and the subsequent chapter underpin everything you do, so check that you can successfully operate with number before you move on. Have you completed the numeracy test form 'Move On'? It might be helpful to do so.

Have you considered looking at some research into mathematics? If you wish to explore in more detail any of the themes developed in this book then log on to the website for the British Society for Research in Mathematics. Here you will be able to gain access to all the latest research on all the topic areas covered in this book. You could reflect on some of the ideas in your portfolio.

Number systems: some background

Just as learning a foreign language is found to help with understanding the construction of one's native tongue, learning about other number systems can be helpful in deepening understanding of our own system.

As far as our records go 3000 BC is the first recorded use of the natural numbers (counting numbers). In most systems developed after that date zero was conceived as an absence of something. However, the ancient Maya civilization did understand this concept so they worked with a different idea of number with units of 20 as the basis for all calculations.

The accepted base commonly adopted is 10. When working with numbers any base can be chosen but 10 happens to be convenient (fingers, toes) and is adopted in our number calculations today.

However, the development of electronic devices which have two states, on or off, has made binary (base 2) useful.

To explain this further:

- In our normal arithmetic 111 means 1×10^2 (hundreds) $+ 1 \times 10$ (tens) $+ 1$ (units).
- In the binary system 111 means $1 \times 2^2 + 1 \times 2 + 1 = 4 + 2 + 1 = 7$ in our 'normal' arithmetic.
- In Mayan mathematics it would be $1 \times 20^2 + 1 \times 20 + 1 = 421$ in our 'normal' arithmetic. They used different symbols, dots and dashes (pebbles and beans).

Ideas and resources on Mayan mathematics can be found on: **www.ncetm.org.uk/resources/14073**.

Review the ideas and resources on this website and highlight those you might use with your learners.

In this book you will find positive and negative whole, fractions, decimals, rational and irrational real numbers. For most calculations we do not have to think about what sort of number it is as the same rules apply.

If you are interested to know more about the history of negative numbers go to:

http://nrich.maths.org/public/viewer.php?obj_id=5961.

Number patterns

An interesting way to explore number patterns is to start with Pascal's triangle shown in Figure 7.1. Can you see how each row of the triangle is constructed by adding the two numbers above? You can add as many rows as you like.

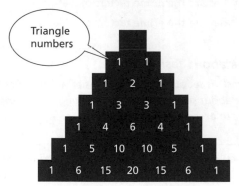

Figure 7.1 Pascal's triangle

Triangle numbers are so named because you can make triangle patterns with, 1, 3, 6, 10 dots, etc.

This pattern is made of 6 dots. Make a triangle pattern using 10 dots.

You can create patterns on Pascal's triangle if you shade, for example, 'multiples of 4', that is 4, 8, 12, etc. or 'square numbers' $1 \times 1 = 1, 2 \times 2 = 4, 3 \times 3 = 9$ etc.

There are many interactive versions of Pascal's triangle online and learners enjoy creating interesting designs which they can save and print.

Prime numbers and factors

The factors of 12 are 1, 2, 3, 4, 6 and 12 itself as each of these numbers divides into 12 a whole number of times.

Prime numbers are numbers that are divisible only by the number itself or 1. 2 is prime, as is 5, but 6 is not because it is also divisible by 2 and 3.

If we wish to find the prime factors of 30 then we start with a pair of factors 6 × 5 and then break down any non-prime into its factors until all the numbers are prime numbers.

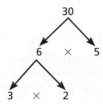

So the prime factors of 30 are 5 × 3 × 2.

Task 7.1

- What are the prime factors of 24?
- What are the prime factors of 240?
- What are the prime factors of 4800?

Think about Task 7. 1

The task as set above becomes easier when presented visually in steps leading to a solution. Think about situations in your working life where the task can be broken down to make it easier to access.

> To see how pharmacists use Pascal's triangle watch the video at:
>
> **www.ncetm.org.uk/resources/13958.**

Operations

There are four operations you use routinely in numeracy: addition, subtraction, multiplication and division.

● Addition and subtraction

You may be familiar with a number line for addition and subtraction of whole number – it is a visual tool to help with addition and subtraction.

You can illustrate that $2 - 4 = -2$ by starting at 2 moving 4 steps to the left or that $-3 + 4 = 1$ by starting at -3 and moving 4 steps to the right. You can also use a line when working with decimals or fractions to illustrate the equivalence of $1\frac{3}{4}$, 1.75 and

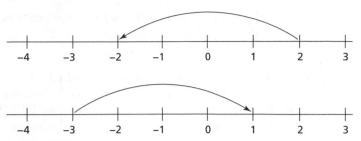

Figure 7.2 Number line

$1\frac{6}{8}$, for example. You need to think in terms of equivalent fractions for addition and subtraction and the process becomes much more obvious if a number line is used to represent the fractions. (See later in this chapter for examples of adding fractions and for multiplication and division of negative numbers.)

● Multiplication

Take the example below which might form part of a food/drink activity in a task set as part of a vocational qualification such as Hospitality and Catering.

Any salesperson would probably instinctively use multiplication alongside addition to work out the total bill. Four beers each £3 and one white wine at £5 a glass requires the calculation: $4 \times 3 + 5 = 17$, to work out the total bill. Prior experience and common sense tells you that the multiplication 4×3 is worked out first to give the total for the beer to which the cost of the wine is added. Even when there is no real-life story behind the calculation, multiplication (and division) take priority over addition or subtraction so that

$$100 - 6 \times 9 = 100 - 54 = 46$$

If you work out 7×13 it is no different from 13×7 because multiplication is *commutative* – it does not matter which way round you arrange the numbers. Choose which makes it easier.

These calculations can be given vocational/work significance to make them more interesting and relevant to your learners. For construction and engineering students number activities around ordering bricks and cement can be designed. The same can apply to resources needed in the working lives of any job in healthcare, media, childcare and the leisure industry.

Moving on to long multiplication, the traditional approach to working out the cost of 17 bread rolls at 39p would be

		3	9
×		1	7
	3	9	0
	2	7	3
	6	6	3

39 is multiplied by 10 and by 7 separately and then the two rows are added together giving an answer of 663p or £6.63.

It is still possible to work out this particular problem mentally if we think of 39 as 40 − 1 so that the calculation becomes

$$40 \times 17 - 1 \times 17 = 680 - 17 = 663$$

This sort of rearrangement becomes increasingly difficult and less worthwhile as the numbers become larger. For 399 × 173 it might be a useful process, but for 173 × 405 it is probably not the best way. Can you see why?

There are alternatives to the traditional method of long multiplication which rely on breaking down the numbers into hundreds, tens, units, etc.

Grid method

The task is the same, to multiply 39 by 17. The first step is to separate the tens and the units and then to multiply each pair together, writing the answer in the appropriate cell. Adding up everything inside 300 + 90 + 210 + 63 gives us the answer 663.

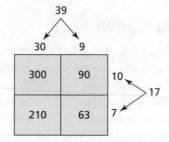

The method can be used with much bigger or much smaller numbers, whole numbers and decimals.

Napier's method

Set up the grid like this for the same calculation 39 × 17.

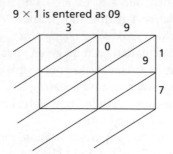

When all the pairs have been multiplied and entered in the grid, the numbers along the diagonals are added to give the total.

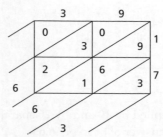

Russian multiplication

This is a different approach which seems a bit strange initially but can be quite efficient.

- Divide the left-hand column by 2 and multiply the right-hand column by 2 until 1 is reached on the left.
- Cross out any rows which have an even number on the left.
- Add up all the remaining numbers on the right to give the answer of 663.

39×17

$\boxed{39 \div 2 = 19 \text{ (remainder 1)}}$

19×34

9×68

~~4×136~~

~~2×272~~

1×544

If you would like to know how it works there are explanations available on the internet.

Difference between two squares

All three methods above would work if the task was to multiply 97 by 103. However, this sum is the same as

$(100 - 3) \times (100 + 3)$

which is quicker to work out as

$100^2 - 3^2 = 10{,}000 - 9 = 9991$

This approach is called the difference between two squares. It is not always an efficient method. It would not be much good for 39×17 as $28^2 - 11^2$ would take as long to work out as the original without a calculator.

Always look for easy solutions to calculations that at first appear complicated.

The traditional and the three alternative approaches work equally well with decimal numbers. Watch the TeacherTube video to see how Scarlett does it:

http://teachertube.com/vicwVideo.php?video_id=12701&title=Grid_Method_Of_Multiplication&vpkey=e257acb1d3&album_id=.

Task 7.2

Beat the Clock

Make up a multiplication question of your own using one three-digit and one two-digit number like 348×76.

- Time yourself in seconds on three different methods. Which one was quicker for you?
- Try a different pair of numbers. Did you use the same method? Did it take the same amount of time?
- What happens to your time if both are three-digit numbers?

Think about Task 7.2

● *What made the method quicker? Was it to do with your skills or with the numbers or method you selected?*

Reflect on this in your learning journal.

● Division

Have you tried using any of these rules? Some may be useful, some may be fun for your students but some may take longer than trying out the division! Decide for yourself which would be useful for you: there are other rules.

● An even number is divisible by **2**.

● If a number has a digit sum of 3, 6, or 9 then it is divisible by **3** (e.g. the digits of 72 add up to 9 so 72 is divisible by 3).

● If a number ends in double zeros then it is divisible by **4** (e.g. 500 = 4 × 12).

● If the last two digits of the number are divisible by **4** then so is the number (e.g. 5084).

● A number that ends in a 0 or a 5 is divisible by **5**.

● Any even number which has a digit sum of 3, 6, or 9 is divisible by **6** (e.g. 72).

● Multiply the last digit by 2 and subtract this figure from the remaining digits. If this number can be divided by 7 then the original would also be divisible by **7** (e.g. 224). 22 − (4 × 2) = 14 which is divisible by 7 so the original number would be 2.

● Any three-digit number with an even first digit and the last two digits divisible by 8 is divisible by **8** (e.g. 616).

● Any number that has a digit sum of **9** can be divided by 9 (e.g. 27).

● Any number that ends in a zero is divisible by **10**.

Learners are likely to have different approaches to division. Repeated subtraction has always been used by some students, but there is some debate about whether 'chunking' is helpful or not.

Long division has never been popular with students. Can you follow the stages in this example to divide 6871 by 16?

$$
\begin{array}{r}
4 \\
16\,\overline{)\,6\;8\;7\;1} \\
-6\;4 \\
\hline
4\;7
\end{array}
$$

$$
\begin{array}{r}
4\;2 \\
16\,\overline{)\,6\;8\;7\;1} \\
-6\;4 \\
\hline
4\;7 \\
-3\;2 \\
\hline
1\;5\;1
\end{array}
$$

```
          4   2   9
  1  6│ 6   8   7   1
     − 6   4
          4   7
        − 3   2
          1   5   1
        − 1   4   4
                  7
```

```
          4   2   9  .4....
  1  6│ 6   8   7   1  .0
     − 6   4
          4   7
        − 3   2
          1   5   1
        − 1   4   4
                  7   0
                − 6   4
                      6
```

If you want to know more about long division have a look at:

www.bbc.co.uk/schools/gcsebitesize/maths/number/

multiplicationdivisionrev2.shtml.

7

Estimation

Estimation is a skill you will more than likely be employing on a regular basis without thinking of it in terms of numeracy.

When you buy a 500g packet of fresh pasta, it tells you how many calories are in both the whole packet and in 125g. It assumes that four people will each eat one quarter of the packet and so the total number of calories and the total weight are each divided by 4.

- If three people each have an equal share their intake would be $500 \div 3 = 166.67$g.
- If two people had really big appetites their intake would each be $500 \div 2 = 250$g, which of course is twice as much as if four shared it.

In the workplace you are likely to use calculators for more challenging questions, but it is important to be able to estimate the answer to check whether or not you have made an error entering the numbers. You will notice that the answers in the pasta example and in the example of long division are no longer whole numbers but decimals. The same basic rules apply and the all the methods illustrated still work, but it is very useful to be able to estimate what the answer is going to be to confirm where the decimal point is placed.

By estimating we know that if three people share the pasta, their portion could not be as big as 1666.7 (more each than if two people eat) or as small as 16.667 (less each than if four people share).

If we needed to work out $493 \div 6.9$ we could estimate this as $490 \div 7 = 70$. When worked out exactly, the answer should be a bit bigger as a smaller number than in the question has been divided by a bigger number than was in the question. In fact, the answer is 71.4, but for many real-life situations an estimate is good enough.

How many 61p wall tiles could you buy with £35.93 if this was all that was left in the budget? We need to work out $35.93 \div 0.61$, which is approximately the same as $36 \div 0.6$, which is the same as $360 \div 6 = 60$. When dividing, the answer is unchanged provided we multiply or divide both the original numbers by the same number, in this case 10. In fact, the answer is 58.9, but we cannot buy bits of tiles so we would have to hope that 58 completed the job! Using the estimate we get a good idea of whether or not we would need to buy a cheaper tile.

$139.5 \div 0.071$ can be estimated by working out $140 \div 0.07$, but this is the same as calculating $14000 \div 7 = 2000$. In fact, the answer is 1964.8 when rounded to one decimal place: we will discuss this in the next chapter on using a calculator.

Fractions

Money and percentages are usually expressed as decimal numbers. The other type of number you are likely to come across fairly frequently is fractions. Working with fractions can cause lots of anxiety but just think about the number and what it represents.

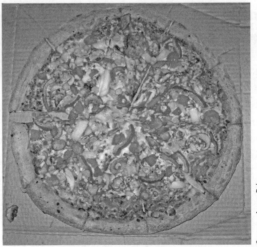

Source: Anne Price

This pizza has been cut into 10 pieces, but not precisely, so each portion is not exactly $\frac{1}{10}$th of the whole. If we could cut it into 20 identical pieces it would be easy to see that $\frac{7}{10}$ is the same as $\frac{14}{20}$.

We could then see that $\frac{1}{4}$ is the same as $\frac{5}{20}$ and that $\frac{7}{10}$ is therefore bigger than $\frac{1}{4}$. Using equivalent fractions allows us to order and compare fractional values.

Cutting it into 16 would show that $\frac{1}{4}$ is the same as $\frac{2}{8}$ or $\frac{4}{16}$. Try folding a circle into halves, quarters and eighths to see the relationship between the fractions.

You may have been taught to multiply top (numerator) and bottom (denominator) by the same number to get an equivalent fraction and of course this method works, but think about why it does.

Suppose we needed to add $\frac{7}{10}$ and $\frac{1}{4}$. We need to think about how we can make them look similar (have the same denominator) so that we can add them together.

$\frac{7}{10}$ is the same as $\frac{14}{20}$

$\frac{1}{4}$ is the same as $\frac{5}{20}$

So we can add $\frac{14}{20}$ and $\frac{5}{20}$ together to get $\frac{19}{20}$

We could work out $\frac{7}{10} - \frac{1}{4}$ in a similar way to get $\frac{14}{20} - \frac{5}{20} = \frac{9}{20}$

Try cutting up paper pizzas to use with learners to show how this works.

Wood sizes in the USA are still provided in inches and centimetres. The table below is adapted from one on an American site.

Table 7.1

Notional All measurements in inches	Actual-Imperial All measurements in inches	Actual-metric All measurements in millimetres
1×2	$\frac{3}{4} \times 1\frac{1}{2}$	19×38
$1\frac{1}{4} \times 4$	$1 \times 3\frac{1}{2}$	25×89
$1\frac{1}{2} \times 6$	$1\frac{1}{4} \times 5\frac{1}{2}$	32×140
2×4	$1\frac{1}{2} \times 3\frac{1}{2}$	38×89
4×4	$3\frac{1}{2} \times 3\frac{1}{2}$	89×89
4×6	$3\frac{1}{2} \times 5\frac{1}{2}$	89×140

2×4s are not actually 2 inches by 4 inches. When the board is first rough-sawn from the log, it is a true 2×4, but it is reduced by the drying process and by being planed to $1\frac{1}{2} \times 3\frac{1}{2}$. Table 7.1 lists some common sizes of timber together with their actual sizes.

So there might be a need to add fractions although many people would choose to use the decimal equivalent or work with the metric measurements.

If we needed to find out the dimensions of 3 pieces of '2 × 4' side by side, it could be

$\left(3 \times 1\frac{1}{2}\right)$ by $3\frac{1}{2}$, that is, $4\frac{1}{2}$ by $3\frac{1}{2}$

or

$\left(3 \times 3\frac{1}{2}\right)$ by $1\frac{1}{2}$, that is, $10\frac{1}{2}$ by $1\frac{1}{2}$

Can you draw a sketch to help you see where the numbers come from? Both of your drawings must represent the same area – we can check by multiplying the lengths of the sides.

$4\frac{1}{2} \times 3\frac{1}{2} = \frac{9}{2} \times \frac{7}{2} = \frac{63}{4} = 15\frac{3}{4}$ $\qquad$ $4\frac{1}{2}$ can be written as 9 halves

81

Try finishing this off

$$10\frac{1}{2} \times 1\frac{1}{2} = \frac{21}{2} \times \frac{3}{2} = \text{?????}$$ How many halves is $3\frac{1}{2}$ the same as?

If we wanted to work out how many pieces of '2 × 4', we would need to create a cross-section of $17\frac{1}{2}$ by $1\frac{1}{2}$, then we would need to divide the fractions

$$\frac{35}{2} \div \frac{7}{2}$$ (*So how many 7s are there in 35?*)

$$\frac{35}{2} \times \frac{2}{7} = \frac{70}{14} = 5$$ Draw a sketch to check.

If you prefer to work with decimals the fractional parts can be changed to decimals by dividing the top number (numerator) by the bottom number (denominator) $15\frac{3}{4}$ would be 15.75 as the whole-number part is 15 and the fraction $\frac{3}{4}$ is changed to a decimal by dividing 3 by 4.

You could try redoing the questions on timber, working with decimals rather than fractions to see which you find easier. Do not forget that many calculators will allow you to enter and calculate with fractional values.

Negative numbers

The number line can help with complex sums but multiplication and division are a bit challenging to understand if solutions are worked out just following the 'two minuses make a positive' rule.

Suppose Joe owed money; suppose he had an overdraft up to his limit of £100 in each of two accounts. If unexpectedly the bank manager says she will cancel the debt because of some error, then Joe is £200 (-2×-100) better off than he was previously.

Division is the inverse of multiplication, so $200 \div -2$ must give us -100 because $-100 \times -2 = 200$.

Task 7.3

When you set up a fish tank you need to work out how many fish you can put into the tank. There are tables like this to help if you know the volume of your tank in litres.

Type of fish	cm/litre
Coldwater	2.5cm/4.5 litre
Tropical	2.5cm/2.25 litre
Marine (reef)	2.5cm/18 litre
Marine (fish only)	5cm/9 litre

For a 360-litre tank, in order to work out how many centimetres of marine fish you are allowed, look at the numbers in the table to see if you use your first answer to work out coldwater/tropical really quickly.

(*continued*)

What would you put in your tank? Look on the internet to find the lengths of different species. Make it an interesting tank!

Source: Anne Price

Think about Task 7.3

- *What mathematical operations have been used to answer this task and in what order?*
- *Could the order have been changed? If so, when was it possible to do so? If not, why not?*

Test yourself

Match up the question and the answer.

Question	Answer
2.1×39	7.5
$-3 \times -2 + 1$	2
$452 \div 90$	6
$2 \times 3 - 5.1$	7
$1.4 + 3.5$	0.9
$15 \div 2$	81.9
$1\frac{3}{4} + 4\frac{1}{4}$	4.9
$5\frac{1}{3} \times \frac{3}{8}$	5.02

Write the answers in order, biggest number first. What sort of number is the difference between the biggest and the smallest?

Going further

- In this chapter we have used the most common forms of numbers but if you are interested you could explore rational and irrational or even imaginary numbers found in the A-level syllabus. The same rules apply! Follow the links on this NCETM page to explore some of these ideas at: **www.ncetm.org.uk/resources/11090**.

- Read a book about pi – there are several available – or listen to BBC Radio 4. See: **www.bbc.co.uk/radio4/science/5numbers2.shtml**.

- Can you write multiplication table squares in bases other than base 10? Help available on: **http://mathforum.org/dr.math/faq/basetables.html#binary**.

Action plan

Having read Chapter 7, what targets will you set yourself? Complete the self-evaluation grid to help you decide. This can be found on the companion website at **www.pearsoned.co.uk/qtls**.

● Self-evaluation

Numeracy skill	*Personal competence*		*Confident in providing opportunities for learners to use this skill*
Number patterns	High (H) Medium(M) Low (L)		H M L
Prime numbers and factors	H M L		H M L
Operations	H M L		H M L
Estimation	H M L		H M L
Fractions	H M L		H M L

● Target setting

Based on your self-evaluation decide on appropriate target(s). Be realistic and set achievable but challenging targets.

Target	*Date for completion*	*Date achieved*
e.g. Introduce the idea of estimation into my teaching sessions.		

Reflections on Chapter 7

- Are you less worried about using the 'right' method? If you wrote down every calculation you did in your head or on paper today, how long would the list be?

- Think about working out whether you had enough money, how much a month extra your pay rise might mean or deciding which filling station to use to fill up with petrol.

7

8 Calculators

Although the use of calculators may be considered controversial by some, today almost everyone uses a calculator whether it be bought for a specific use or be conveniently available for use as an additional function on equipment such as a computer or mobile phone.

This chapter encourages you to learn more about the range of possible uses for calculators while also offering guidance in areas of numeracy not yet discussed, such as percentages.

By the end of this chapter you will understand:

- Different types of calculators.
- BODMAS.
- Percentages.
- Raising to a power.
- Rounding.

The minimum core standards for numeracy covered in this chapter are:
N1 L2.5
N2 L2.7 L2.8 L2.9

Calculators in everyday use

A simple four-function calculator performs the basic arithmetic operations: add (+), subtract (−), multiply (×), and divide (÷), whereas a scientific version will have many more built-in functions. Some will include statistical functions allowing you to easily obtain values for the mean, etc. More elaborate calculators will have graph functions which enable the completion of complex calculations.

First look at your calculator, glance through the instruction booklet if you have one to get a sense of what type it might be. You can also access calculators online from a range of sources.

i-Google has an online calculator which can be added to your homepage at no cost. This calculator has more functions than the basic 4/5 calculator, but less than a scientific one.

Those of you using a Windows® operating system for your computer will be able to access a calculator by opening up the start menu and using the search function to find a calculator. You may wish to bookmark this so that is appears on your desktop every time you start up your computer.

Figure 8.1 shows the front face of what is described as a *standard* calculator. Figure 8.2 shows a *scientific* calculator. These are the two types most likely to be useful to you.

Figure 8.1 A standard calculator

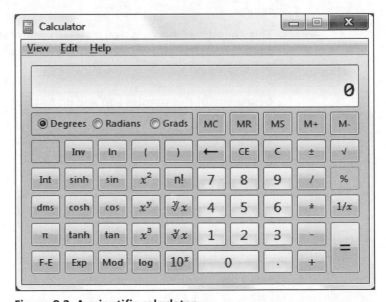

Figure 8.2 A scientific calculator

Source: Microsoft product screenshots reprinted with permission from Microsoft Corporation

Order of operations

The acronym used to describe what is known as 'order of operations' is BODMAS:

Brackets, **O**ther, **D**ivision and **M**ultiplication, **A**ddition and **S**ubtraction.

BODMAS is worth remembering since it helps us to know the order in which certain mathematical functions need to be performed.

For example: To work out $4 + 2 \times 5$ we must carry out the multiplication first, so $4 + 10 = 14$.

If our key presses on the standard calculator are

$$\boxed{4} \quad \boxed{+} \quad \boxed{2} \quad \boxed{*} \quad \boxed{5}$$

we get the incorrect answer 30.

The scientific calculator gives us the correct answer of 14 because such calculators have what some manufacturers call VPAM – **V**isually **P**erfect **A**lgebraic **M**ethod – or, alternatively, Natural Display.

To use the standard calculator correctly we have to change the order of key presses so that the multiplication is carried out before the addition.

$$\boxed{2} \quad \boxed{*} \quad \boxed{5} \quad \boxed{+} \quad \boxed{4}$$

Another example of the importance of BODMAS would be to evaluate $5 + \sqrt{16}$ (5 added to the square root of 16) which we can work out in our heads to be $5 + 4 = 9$.

On the standard calculator we have to put the instruction to square root after the number, so the key presses are

$$\boxed{5} \quad \boxed{+} \quad \boxed{16} \quad \boxed{\sqrt{}} \quad \boxed{=}$$

However, the scientific calculator reads the task correctly. It allows for squaring a number ($3^2 = 9$) or raising it to any power ($3^7 = 2187$) without performing repeated multiplication.

The key presses to work out 3^2 (3×3) would be

$$\boxed{3} \quad \boxed{x^2} \quad \boxed{=}$$

To work out 3^7 the keys would be

$$\boxed{3} \quad \boxed{x^y} \quad \boxed{7} \quad \boxed{=}$$

which is much easier than $3 \times 3 \times 3 \times 3 \times 3 \times 3 \times 3$.

Suppose we wished to calculate $4.2 \div (2 - 1.85)^2$. This is easily computed by a scientific calculator since such calculators allow for the use of brackets, so the question can be typed in as it appears, to give the answer 186.67. Check that you can get this answer on your calculator, remembering BODMAS.

Other uses

Let us use either calculator to compare two cars. We will use percentages in the calculations to compare their output.

Model	A	B
Capacity	2976cc	4163cc
Power	220hp	344hp
Weight	1580kg	1660kg
0–60mph	7.7sec	5.3sec

With this information available we can work out, for example, the difference in capacity between B and A. To do this the key presses would be:

Be careful to use the substraction symbol

Answer = 1187.

If we needed to know what the capacity of A is relative to B as a percentage, we would work out

The symbol could be × or * for multiplication and/or ÷ for division.

To one decimal place this would be 71.5%.

- Although some calculators do have percentage buttons (%), it is better for your students to think about the calculation they are performing.
- Unless we press equals after the first calculation, some calculators may not 'understand' to multiply the answer by 100.
- If the answer had been 100%, then cars A and B would have had identical capacities.
- If 50%, then A's capacity would be half of B's.
- A sports car may have 200% of the capacity of a small hatchback.

Supposing we knew that car A did 41 miles to the gallon on average. How many litres would it need to travel 220 miles?

The number of gallons would be 220 divided by 41. The number of litres would be the answer multiplied by 4.5 as this is the number of litres in a gallon.

$$\boxed{220} \quad \boxed{\div} \quad \boxed{41} \quad \boxed{=} \quad \boxed{\times} \quad \boxed{4.5} \quad \boxed{=}$$

Answer = 24.15 litres

The answer has been rounded to two decimal places but we would probably just use 24 in everyday life. This would only be a problem if we did not have a little more in the tank!

If A's fuel tank could hold 35 litres it would need to be $\frac{24.15}{35} \times 100\%$ full at least. Do you agree that this works out to be 69% full?

What does the fuel gauge on your car look like when the tank is nearly 70% full?

These calculations could be included in a Leisure and Tourism activity, in a business plan for the costs of running a fleet of company cars and in a number of other vocational contexts.

The example below might be used in a Food and Nutrition qualification, in a Healthcare qualification or in any business, leisure or retail environment where food is provided.

Task 8.1

A typical lasagne is composed of food categories as in the table.

Lasagne		
Calories	570	
	Quantity	% daily value
Total fat	30 g	46%
Sat. fat	13 g	65%
Sodium	1670 mg	70%
Total carbs	45 g	15%
Sugars	11 g	
Protein	29 g	

To work out how many grammes of saturated fat is a typical daily amount we would calculate $\frac{30}{46} \times 100$ ($\frac{30}{46}$ gives us a value for 1% which we can then multiply by 100).

In the same way work out how much sodium and fibre we should consume in a day.

Find out what the recommended intake is for an adult male and an adult female and calculate what percentage of the daily calorie intake this lasagne represents.

Think about Task 8.1

● *Without a calculator how easy would it have been to complete these calculations? Perhaps estimation would have helped? Instead of 46% we could have used an estimate of 50% and then doubled the number of grammes of fat.*

● Body mass index

To work out your body mass index:

- Work out your height in metres.
- Measure your weight in kilograms.
- Divide the weight by the height squared.

So if you are 1.75 metres tall and weigh 70 kg using a scientific calculator the key presses would be

$$\boxed{70} \quad \boxed{\div} \quad \boxed{1.75} \quad \boxed{x^2} \quad \boxed{=} \quad \boxed{22.9}$$

giving an answer of 22.9.

Task 8.2

Underweight	BMI less than 18.5
Ideal	18.5–25
Overweight	25–30
Obese	30–40
Very obese	greater than 40

- How would a person 1.8 metres tall weighing 71 kg be described?
- What about a 1.5 metres 57 kg woman?
- How many kilogrammes (approximately) would the first person have gained if six months later he was described as just overweight?

● Rounding

This has been touched upon already. Mostly it is common sense. Look at these petrol prices.

UK petrol prices for Thursday 4th Feb 2010

	Min.	Max.
Unleaded	107.9 p	123.9 p
Diesel	108.9 p	127.0 p
LRP	111.9 p	119.9 p
Super	111.9 p	129.9 p
LPG	52.9 p	69.9 p

The average price of unleaded on this day was 112.1 p but we have no coin for 0.1 p. When we look at the answer we decide how accurately we need to know from a common-sense point of view. It is in a garage's interest to price to one decimal place because we buy many litres at a time but we would be less impressed if a supermarket advertised meat at £7.567 per kilo.

> The BBC site explains the detail:
> **www.bbc.co.uk/schools/ks3bitesize/maths/number/approximation/revise4.shtml**.

It a good idea to practise a few: check that you agree with the numbers in each column.

Original	To two decimal places	To one decimal place	To one significant figure
23.476	23.48	23.5	20
1.875	1.88	1.9	2
231.342	231.34	231.3	200
4.3875	4.39	4.4	4
13.867	13.87	13.9	10
0.0567	0.06	0.1	0.06
0.00896	0.01	0.0	0.009

Check to make sure you understand why.

The skills used above are relevant and important for success in everyday life as well as for success in a range of vocational areas.

8

Task 8.3

Think about the calculations you have carried out today with/without a calculator.

Consider how accurately you needed to know the answer. To one decimal place?

Think about each of the following:

- Measurements of a room.
- Diameter of a pipe.
- Machining an engine part.
- Weighing flour for a cake.
- Adding water to pastry.
- Timing a race.

How accurately do you need to know the measurement? The same ideas apply when deciding how to round the answer provided on a calculator.

If we cut a 3-metre plank into 7 equal parts, each will be 0.428571428 metres long! Would thinking of each piece as 43 centimetres be good enough or could this cause a problem? If we used 40 (one significant figure), then we might be wasting materials. What would you do and why?

Test yourself

1 Estimate 1.49 − 0.16 × 9.89. Work out your answer on a calculator.

2 (1.3 + 2.6)2 − 1.2 × 4.

3 Use your calculator to work out how much money you would have after six months if you started with £250 and got

　a. 2.3% interest per month – you get interest on your interest

　b. 4.65% interest added every two months.

● Using the power button is the most efficient way to calculate these.

● No rounding until you get to your final answer.

Going further

● 'Calculating the Difference: A Discussion of the Use of Calculators in the English Primary Classroom'. Although this article is set in a primary context it makes interesting reading: **http://nrich.maths.org/2553**.

● Watch this Maths at Work video about running budgets: **www.ncetm.org.uk/resources/9685**.

● Explore the use of a graphic calculator – borrow one from the Mathematics department. It can be fun!

Action plan

Having read Chapter 8, what targets will you set yourself? Complete the self-evaluation grid to help you decide. This can be found on the companion website at **www.pearsoned.co.uk/qtls**.

● Self-evaluation

Numeracy skill	Personal competence			Confident in providing opportunities for learners to use this skill		
BODMAS	High (H)	Medium (M)	Low (L)	H	M	L
Percentages	H	M	L	H	M	L
Raising to a power	H	M	L	H	M	L
Rounding	H	M	L	H	M	L

● Target setting

Based on your self-evaluation, decide on appropriate target(s). Be realistic and set achievable but challenging targets.

Target	Date for completion	Date achieved
e.g. Provide students with the opportunity to discuss how they use their calculator.		

Reflections on Chapter 8

- Think about the times you use a calculator and the reasons for doing so. Sometimes it might be for security. You may well be able to work out the answer to the required level of accuracy without the need to use a calculator.
- Ask your students how they decide whether or not to use a calculator.

8

9 Common measures

The most common measures you will meet are time, length, mass, temperature and capacity, but there may be others that are particular to your own subject area. Engineers are likely to use pressure, energy, velocity, density, and measures of rotation and force.

This chapter is a reminder of the units you are likely to be using. There are more tasks in this section than in other chapters, but each one is quick to do and encourages you to think about how you might be using common measures in your teaching and professional practice.

By the end of this chapter you will understand:

- Time.
- Temperature.
- Length/distance.
- Speed/velocity.
- Capacity/volume.
- Mass/weight.
- Density.
- Rotation.

The minimum core standards for numeracy to referred in this chapter are:
MSS1   L2.2   L2.3   L2.4   L2.5   L2.6

Time

Time influences everything we do and your learners will find this to be case whatever vocational area they choose to work in. Hair colourants cannot be left on the client's head too long, cakes must be removed from the oven at the right moment and athletes strive to complete the race in ever-decreasing time intervals. In these and other cases our measurements will be in hours or minutes, but for business plans or building projects we may be more concerned about what happens over days, weeks and months. The swimmer may be concerned to improve his time by fractions of a second. We move naturally between these units to work in measurements which are appropriate and easiest to work with.

For example, a journey to the moon might take five days.

- A day on the moon lasts 29.5 of our Earth days.
- An Earth day is 24 hours or $24 \times 60 = 1440$ minutes or $1440 \times 60 = 86,400$ seconds.
- A moon day is 708 hours or 42,400 minutes or 2,548,800 seconds.

We work in both the 12-hour and the 24-hour clock using 6.30pm and 1800 hours interchangeably.

While time intervals are the same wherever you are in the world, the time of day varies. So you can 'gain' or 'lose' time according to the direction you travel.

Time plays an important part in our lives. It features when planning trips abroad, for attendance at business meetings, conferences and holidays.

Your learners will need to be able to read timetables, use the 24-hour clock and plan schedules to ensure complex tasks are completed on time.

When planning a complicated meal, such as Christmas lunch, it might be helpful to prepare a work schedule to make sure that the turkey gets cooked thoroughly but that the sprouts are not overcooked.

Task 9.1

Think of a complex task that you expect your students to undertake over a period of hours or days.

Consider how producing a schedule might assist them. It requires that the time for each task is either known or can be estimated – like cooking or journey times. Receptionists at hair and beauty salons must be constantly making such decisions.

Temperature

The most common measure of temperature in the UK is degrees Celsius, °C. Examples would be

- Temperatures in big-freeze Britain plunged below minus 21°C as the country suffered its coldest night of the winter so far.
- The UK has seen its hottest day of the year so far with temperatures reaching 27°C.

- The average human body temperature is 37°C.
- The boiling point of water is considered to be 100°C.

Some countries, notably the United States, continue to use Fahrenheit: International Falls, Minnesota is the coldest city with a mean temperature of 36.4°F. At first glance this may seem hotter than our warmest day so it is important to read the units and realise that a Fahrenheit measurement has been used here.

It is possible to convert from one measurement system to the other easily.

● To convert Fahrenheit into Celsius

- Subtract 32 from the Fahrenheit number.
- Divide the answer by 9.
- Multiply that answer by 5.

For example, to convert 95°F to Celsius:

$$95 - 32 = 63.$$
$$63 \div 9 = 7.$$
$$7 \times 5 = 35° \text{ C}.$$

● To convert Celsius temperatures into Fahrenheit

- Multiply the Celsius temperature by 9.
- Divide the answer by 5.
- Add 32.

Can you show that 20°C is 68°F?

Task 9.2

This table records the weather in January. Use the table to answer the following questions.

	Minimum	Maximum
Jan 8th	16°C	34°C
Jan 9th	22°C	34°C
Jan 10th	17°C	33°C
Jan 11th	19°C	41°C
Jan 12th	23°C	29°C

- Which day has the biggest difference between maximum and minimum temperatures? Which day the least?
- Guess what the figures would be if the table represented UK weather. Check with values found on the internet.

Think about Task 9.2

- *Are there occasions when you need to be aware of the room temperature as it may have an effect on the topic you are teaching/demonstrating?*
- *When you measure temperature how accurately do you do so? Is to the nearest degree good enough?*

Length

In the chapter on shape and space you will find several references to length. The most common unit in Mathematics textbooks is centimetres, but in your subject area this may not be so. We have access to a range of possible units, but using the metric system the connection between the units is always a power of 10. The conversions used most routinely are:

10 millimetres = 1 centimetre

100 centimetres = 1 metre

1000 metres = 1 kilometre

but the prefix kilo-, centi-, etc. can be used with other metric measurements. Table 9.1 shows you how other units relate to the unit of one metre.

Table 9.1 Conversion to 1 metre

Prefix		How many times bigger than 1 metre	Multiply by
Yotta-	Y	10^{24}	1 000 000 000 000 000 000 000 000
Zetta-	Z	10^{21}	1 000 000 000 000 000 000 000
Exa-	E	10^{18}	1 000 000 000 000 000 000
Peta-	P	10^{15}	1 000 000 000 000 000
Tera-	T	10^{12}	1 000 000 000 000
Giga-	G	10^{9}	1 000 000 000
Mega-	M	10^{6}	1 000 000
myria-	my	10^{4}	10 000 (this is now obsolete)
kilo-	k	10^{3}	1000
hecto-	h	10^{2}	100
deka-	da	10	10
—	—	—	—
deci-	d	10^{-1}	0.1
centi-	c	10^{-2}	0.01
milli-	m	10^{-3}	0.001
micro-	u (mu)	10^{-6}	0.000 001
nano-	n	10^{-9}	0.000 000 001
pico-	p	10^{-12}	0.000 000 000 001
femto-	f	10^{-15}	0.000 000 000 000 001
atto-	a	10^{-18}	0.000 000 000 000 000 001
zepto-	z	10^{-21}	0.000 000 000 000 000 000 001
yocto-	y	10^{-24}	0.000 000 000 000 000 000 000 001

If your interest is electronics, you may be using both very large and very small units. Think about the file size of a digital photograph compared with a Word document.

Task 9.3

We use the term *distance* when describing journey length.

Below you will see a table of directions, similar to ones you would find in Google Maps, for travel across Paris. How long is the journey in total? You will need to change all the measurements into kilometres or all into metres.

When do you think Google changes from giving distances in km to distances in metres?

Musée du Louvre to Arc de Triomphe

1	Head **south** on **Place du Carrousel** toward **Quai François Mitterrand**	120 m
2	**Place du Carrousel** turns slightly **left** and becomes **Pont du Carrousel**	180 m
3	Turn **right** to stay on **Pont du Carrousel**	21 m
4	Slight **right** at **Quai Voltaire**	240 m
5	Continue onto **Quai Anatole France**	850 m
6	Turn **right** at **Pont de la Concorde**	180 m
7	Continue onto **Place de la Concorde**	270 m
8	Slight **left** to stay on **Place de la Concorde**	78 m
9	Slight **right** to stay on **Place de la Concorde**	110 m
10	Continue onto **Avenue des Champs-Elysées**	1.7 km
11	Slight **right** to stay on **Avenue des Champs-Élysées**	300 m
12	**Avenue des Champs-Élysées** turns **left** and becomes **Avenue de la Grande Armée.** Destination will be on the left	14 m

9

Think about Task 9.3

● *In your own subject area you will use a range of units of length. What determines the unit you use?*

Velocity/speed

Both velocity and speed are measures of distance travelled over a period of time, so typical units are metres per second or kilometres per hour. The difference is that when the term 'velocity' is used, the direction is also known (and stated).

Capacity/volume

Capacity is a term used to describe how much a container can hold with units such as litres. Volume refers to how much space an object displaces and is measured in units such as cubic metres.

● 1 cubic metre is equivalent to 1000 litres.

● 1000 cubic centimetres is equivalent to 1 litre.

Cans of drink are usually 330 millilitres (ml) or 0.33 litres (l): the same prefixes can be used as for length.

Task 9.4

The shampoos listed below are designed for cleaning cars. To use you have to dilute the shampoo as suggested.

A   15 ml to 10 l of water
B   25 ml to 20 l of water
C   75 ml to 20 l of water

● Which is the most concentrated?
● How many litres of diluted car wash would a 250ml bottle of each make?

Think about Task 9.4

● *Look on your shelves and compare the capacities of the containers stored. Is it just liquids that are labelled in this way?*
● *Design a task specifically for your vocational subject area which requires your learners to demonstrate an understanding of volume/capacity.*

Mass

Although we use *mass* and *weight* as interchangeable terms in everyday language, the mass of an object is how much matter it contains and is measured in grammes (g) or kilograms (kg); the weight of an object is the force caused by gravity pulling down on the mass of an object and is measured in newtons (N).

The mass of an object is the same wherever it is placed but the same item would weigh differently on the moon.

So, when we are using a recipe it is actually the mass of each ingredient that is listed. This recipe for scones uses measures of mass (grammes) and capacity (millilitres)

● 225 g self-raising flour
● 55 g butter
● 25 g caster sugar
● 150 ml milk

Can you think of other situations where units of capacity and of mass are used in the same process?

Density

If we know both the mass and the volume of something, we can work out a value for its density:

Density = mass ÷ volume,

and so it is usually measured in grammes per cubic centimetre.

The density of water varies with temperature but is usually considered to be 1 gramme/cubic centimetre.

Aluminium has a lower density than steel so cars made of aluminium are likely to be lighter than those made of steel.

Task 9.5

Do you work with any of these metals?

Metal	Density g/cm³
Gold	19.3
Silver	10.5
Platinum	21.4
Palladium	12.0
Copper	9.0

If not, find out what the density is of the materials you work with on a daily basis.

You can do so by looking on the internet or by finding the mass of a particular volume of piping, shampoo, jam, etc. Are you surprised by your results?

Rotation

We measure rotation in degrees. If we turn through a whole circle then we have turned through 360°. So, if we are facing north and turn around until we are again facing north, we will have moved through 360°.

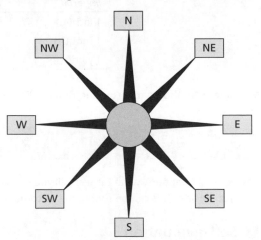

The angle between east and west is 180°: between S and SW is 45°.

Have a look at these sites to see how rotation is converted into linear energy:
- **www.flying-pig.co.uk/mechanisms/pages/rackandpinion.html**
- **www.flying-pig.co.uk/mechanisms/pages/pulley.html**.

Test yourself

You may wish to use the activity below to test your understanding. In addition you may wish to design something similar to use with your students.

Fill in the missing words.

At 2 .... Jo went to fill up her car with petrol. The price per .... was £1.10 but as the tank had a .... of 35 .... it was quite an expensive trip. She decided that she needed a few bits and pieces so bought 500 .... of butter, a 370 .... jar of jam and a loaf of bread.

The garage was only 2 .... from home but it was a slow journey back taking 20 .... She worked out that her average .... was only 6 ....

5 .... after getting home at 1455 .... Jo sat down to her afternoon snack. Well, at least I was only at the garage for .... she thought.

Going further

- Find out more about forces at: www.bbc.co.uk/scotland/learning/bitesize/higher/physics/ mech_matt/forces_rev1.shtml, or pressure at: www.bbc.co.uk/scotland/learning/bitesize/ higher/physics/mech_matt/pressure_rev2.shtml
- Explore how to convert metric measures into imperial measures. This table will start you off but you will be able to find interactive tools on the internet.

Imperial	Metric
1 inch(in)	2.54 cm
1 foot (ft)	0.3048 m
1 yard(yd)	0.9144 m

- Angles can also be measured in radians. Find out what a radian is.

Action plan

Having read Chapter 9, what targets will you set yourself? Complete the self-evaluation grid to help you decide. This can be found on the companion website at **www.pearsoned.co.uk/qtls**.

● Self-evaluation

Numeracy skill	Personal competence			Confident in providing opportunities for learners to use this skill		
Time	High (H)	Medium (M)	Low (L)	H	M	L
Temperature	H	M	L	H	M	L

(continued)

Numeracy skill	Personal competence			Confident in providing opportunities for learners to use this skill		
Length/distance	H	M	L	H	M	L
Speed/velocity	H	M	L	H	M	L
Capacity/volume	H	M	L	H	M	L
Mass/weight	H	M	L	H	M	L
Density	H	M	L	H	M	L
Rotation	H	M	L	H	M	L

● Target setting

Based on your self-evaluation, decide on appropriate target(s). Be realistic and set achievable but challenging targets.

Target	Date for completion	Date achieved
e.g. to encourage my students to think about time zones, e.g. *What would be the latest date/time they could leave London to be in Sydney for New Year?*		

9

Reflections on Chapter 9

Is there anything else needed other than what is shown in the picture on the right to obtain a value for each of the common measures discussed in this chapter?

Some might not be sophisticated or accurate enough for your purpose. What do you use instead? Surveyors use lasers. For some purposes it is not essential to measure accurately, for others it is crucial. List the measuring tasks you set your students and think about how precise they need to be.

Source: Anre Price

10 Shape and space

This chapter, focusing on shape and space, provides the underpinning mathematical ideas and knowledge for you to think about and explore. It does not seek to cover everything in depth but to encourage you to consider how much you already use the concepts in an everyday setting. Throughout, you will be encouraged to relate ideas to your own specialist area and look for particular instances of real-world examples in the application of geometry.

Tasks have been included to be used by individuals or worked on as a collaborative activity: the learning is much deeper when working collaboratively.

By the end of this chapter you will understand:

- 2D and 3D shapes and their properties.
- Perimeter, area and volume and units of measurement.
- Dimensions and proportions.
- Transformations.
- Scale drawing.

The minimum core standards for numeracy referred to in this chapter are:

MSS1   **L2.7**   **L2.8**   **L2.9**   **L2.10**

MSS2   **L2.1**   **L2.2**   **L2.3**

N1   **L2.4**

Background information

We are surrounded by 2D and 3D shapes which we have no problem in describing in our everyday lives. We all know what a can looks like. Mathematics requires us to be more precise in our application of terms and gives us specific language to apply, using cylinder for can, rectangle for oblong, and square only when it is exactly square.

There are occasions when using the correct word is vital. For example, in physics we have to be careful how we use the terms 'mass' and 'weight'; in everyday life it really does not matter.

2D and 3D shapes and their properties

Each mathematical shape has particular properties; these are some examples.

● Triangles have three sides.

- An equilateral triangle has three equal sides, three equal angles and three lines of symmetry.

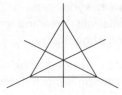

- An isosceles triangle has two equal sides and two equal angles and just one line of symmetry.

● A quadrilateral has four sides.
- A rectangle has two pairs of equal sides and all its angles are 90 degrees. It has two lines of symmetry.

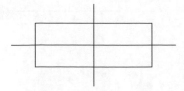

– A square has four equal sides and four right angles. It has four lines of symmetry.

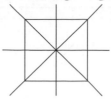

● A circle has an infinitive number of sides. Think of it as a regular polygon with too many sides to count. It has an infinite number of lines of symmetry.

These 3D shapes are prisms because they have the same cross section throughout their length. A straight section of copper piping would be a prism.

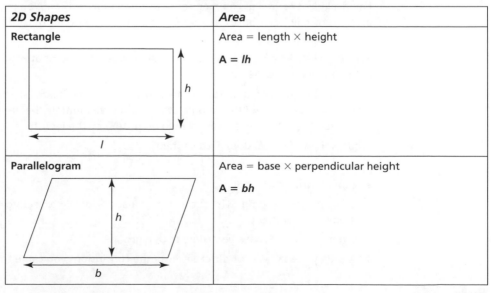

Rectangular prism   **Hexagonal prism**

Perimeter, area and volume and units of measurement

Perimeter is the word used to describe the distance around the outside of a shape, so it is measured in centimetres, metres, etc. The area is the space inside measured in centimetres squared. Volume is measured in centimetres cubed. When talking about capacity, the unit used is usually litres.

The formulae below will help to remind you how to work out areas.

10

2D Shapes	Area
Rectangle 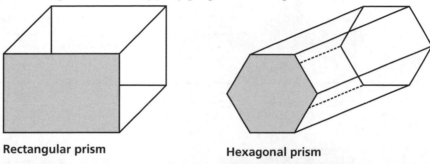	Area = length × height **A = *lh***
Parallelogram	Area = base × perpendicular height **A = *bh***

2D Shapes	Area
Triangle	Area = half base × perpendicular height **A = ½ bh** So, if a triangle has a base of 10cm and a height of 8cm then the area is ½ × 10 × 8 = 40cm²
Circle	Area = pi × the radius squared **A = πr^2** So a circle of radius 14cm has an area of 22/7 × 14 × 14 = 616cm² π = 3.14 or 22/7

Task 10.1

As you go through this task, make a list of all the units you have used or become aware of.

Next time you are at the supermarket find the aisle with cereal in it.

- Is all cereal packed in cuboids?

- Look at those that are not.

- What properties does the packaging have in common with cuboids?

Why do you think the manufacturer has opted for this packaging? Try to use mathematical ideas as well as common sense to come to a decision. You might want to look at issues of filling the boxes, stacking on shelves, the amount of card used to construct the packaging, etc.

You could pause here but you may decide that this is the point at which you need more data and take some measurements.

For at least three cuboids measure the length, width, and height so that you can calculate the volume. To find the volume of any prism we multiply the area of cross-section (the shaded section in the prisms shown on p. 109) by the length.

What weight of cereal does each contain?

- Are you surprised?

- Explain why or why not.

- Compare your findings with those of a colleague, ideally collecting everyone's measurements together.

- What conclusions have you come to as a group?

- Are they the same as or different from the conclusions you came to on your own?

Think about Task 10.1

- *What did you learn that surprised you?*
- *What did you learn about working collaboratively?*
- *If you are interested in knowing more about collaborative approaches, details of the jigsaw method are provided in the Appendix on p. 140.*

Task 10.2

Doors

Source: Anne Price

10

- Think about the doors you walk through.
- In what ways are they the same as the doors in the pictures?
- In what ways are they different?
- Try to describe the shapes as precisely as you can.

Most of these doors are composite shapes, made up of two or more mathematical shapes, perhaps rectangles and semicircles. How would you find the area of this door? How might this activity be adapted for your vocational area?

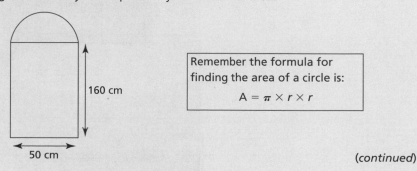

160 cm

50 cm

Remember the formula for finding the area of a circle is:

$$A = \pi \times r \times r$$

(continued)

What about doors with glass panels like these?

Source: Anne Price

One door has a significantly larger proportion of glass. Why would this matter?

In Engineering and Construction classes a number of fact-finding mathematical activities can be developed around these ideas linking, if appropriate, with energy efficiency values.

Think about Task 10.2

Think about how you divided up each shape into glass and wood. The difference in materials made it easier to break down the task.

- *Could you use colour/texture or other properties to help students to do the same?*
- *'Doors are designed for predominately practical reasons'. Do you agree?*

Dimensions and proportions

This washbasin has a circular cross section when viewed from above. Do you think its shape was chosen for practical or aesthetic reasons? Why do you think this?

Source: Anne Price

You might come to a different decision if you had to consider the volume of the basin but we do not have any measurements to work this out.

Is there a minimum volume of water which would make a washbasin useful?

Any design process requires a balance between practicality and aesthetic appeal. Mathematics can help with both!

Credit cards, Oyster cards, etc. are rectangles with sides in the ratio of the golden ratio 1.618:1, which is supposed to be aesthetically pleasing. Maybe it encourages us to use them more!

> If you would like to know more about the golden ratio, go to
>
> **www.bbc.co.uk/radio4/science/5numbers3.shtml**.

The pyramids of Giza provide one of the earliest uses of the golden ratio in architecture, but through the centuries there are many other famous examples.

Are there examples from your own subject area when learners might use this ratio perhaps without realising? Examples can be found of its use in fashion, furniture and music as well as in architecture.

Mathematical 'facts'

Mathematics requires that when we use facts like the angle properties of circles, that they have been proved in a rigorous way. These theorems provide the basis for deeper mathematical understanding. The one which you will be most familiar with is likely to be that of Pythagoras. Did you know that the grounds person at your college probably uses it to make sure that the angles of the pitch are in fact right angles? Why not ask him/her how he/she does this? Useful on building sites too.

Here is a reminder of Pythagoras's theorem:

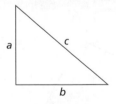

$$c^2 = a^2 + b^2$$

In this triangle

$b = 8$ and $a = 6$ so
$c^2 = 6^2 + 8^2$
$c^2 = 36 + 64$
$c^2 = 100$
$c = 10$

Widescreen television screens have sides in the ratio 16 to 9. What would be the length of the sides of a 37-inch screen? You could measure one to check your answer.

If you are interested you can find interactive demonstrations of Pythagoras's theorem on the internet. You can also find more formal proofs.

Transformation of shapes

Shapes may be moved and appear altered. In everyday language we refer to *rotation*, *reflection* and *translation*. When working mathematically we are required to introduce more precision. In the diagram below the shaded area of the shape has been rotated through 90 degrees anti-clockwise about (0, 0). To describe the transformation we need three specific pieces of information: (1) rotate, (2) the angle of rotation and the nature of the movement, whether it be clockwise or anti-clockwise, and (3) the point about which it is rotated.

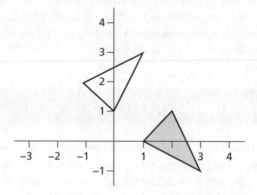

The diagram below shows enlargement of the smaller quadrilateral by scale factor 3 centre (0, 0).

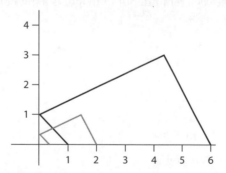

When we speak mathematically, *translation* refers to moving a shape across the page so that it remains unchanged in shape and size. We specify the move as a vector such as $\binom{3}{4}$ which means 3 units across to the right and 4 up. Vector $\binom{-3}{-4}$ means 3 units to the left and 4 down.

Many tile patterns in kitchens, for example, are created through a process of mathematical transformation. These ideas are relevant to all aspects of design whether for kitchen tiling, wallpapering or fashion.

Can you identify what transformations have been used in the examples shown below?

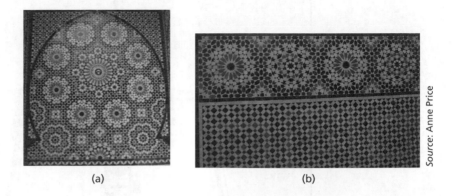

(a)   (b)

Source: Anne Price

Look around you and you will see many more examples, carpet and curtain design, etc.

Scale drawing

It is impossible to think about constructing something significant without first producing a plan. The more accurate the plan, the more useful it is likely to be especially when trying to convey the same information to a number of individuals: for example, building a house or landscaping a garden.

Below you will see a scale drawing of a swimming pool from the top (plan view). It does not state what scale has been used, which makes it less useful because we might want to know other dimensions which have not been listed. We can work out the scale by measuring the length on the plan and dividing the actual length by this value.

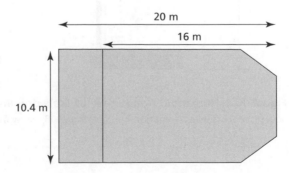

Maps always have a scale. Have a look at Google Maps on the internet. Can you find your home? Note how the scale changes as you zoom in and out.

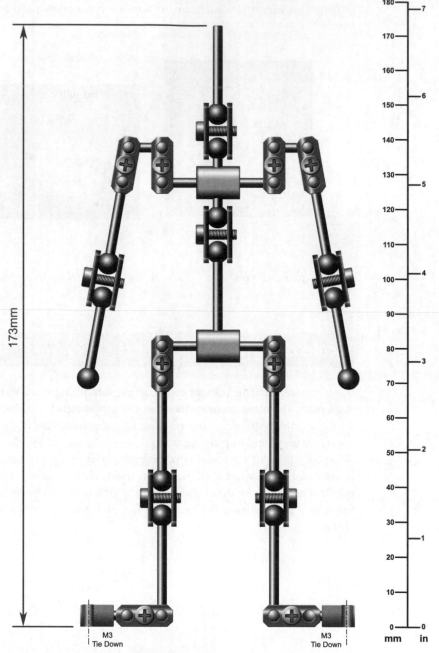

Figure 10.1 Humanoid Armature R101 scale drawing
Source: Mark Reeve Animation Engineering 2008, www.markreeve.co.uk

Task 10.3

Figure 10.1 shows a scale drawing of an armature which is particularly humanoid! It is used in puppetry. Measure the length of the limbs on this diagram.

● If the height of the armature represents an average human male would the limbs also be average? Justify your argument. (You will need to look on the internet to find values for average height, etc.)

● Do you think K9 could be considered as a scale model of a dog?

Test yourself

Try these questions and check your answers. If there are any you are not sure about then make sure you include the topic in your action plan.

1 Draw the triangle with vertices (0, 4) (3, 0) and (4, 5).
   a. Reflect the triangle in the x axis.
   b. Enlarge the new triangle scale factor 2 centre (0, 0).

2 A shape is 4 units high, has a surface area of 8 square units and a volume of 12 cubic units.
   a. What units might be used? Think of at least two examples.
   b. If a similar shape (exactly the same proportions, just a different size) is 10 units high, how big a surface area does it have? What about its volume?

3 A staircase consists of 12 steps 10 cm high and 15 cm across. A piece of timber is fitted from the bottom of the first step to the top of the last step. How long is the piece of timber?

4 A salon has mirrors which are hexagonal in shape (and regular). How many lines of symmetry does each mirror have?

10

Going further

This section offers a few possibilities to take your ideas further.

● Explore The National Centre for Excellence in Teaching Mathematics (NCETM) at **www.ncetm.org.uk/home** which offers resources, on line courses and workshops.

● Read John Dabell's article 'The hole truth' in the *Times Educational Supplement*, February 2008 Issue 4773, special section p. 47. Write any thoughts you have in your ILP.

● Watch Open University programmes to give you an understanding of where and when some of these ideas of geometry originated. See: **www.open2.net/storyofmaths/index. html**.

● Read *Models of Learning: Tools for Teaching* by Bruce Joyce, Emily Calhoun and David Hopkins to learn about other approaches to teaching.

Action plan

Having read Chapter 10, what targets will you set yourself? Complete the self-evaluation grid to help you decide. This can be found on the companion website at **www.pearsoned. co.uk/qtls**.

● Self-evaluation

Numeracy skill	Personal competence			Confident in providing opportunities for learners to use this skill		
Properties of shapes	High (H)	Medium (M)	Low (L)	H	M	L
Perimeter, area and volume	H	M	L	H	M	L
Pythagoras's theorem*	H	M	L	H	M	L
Transformations	H	M	L	H	M	L
Scale	H	M	L	H	M	L

*Beyond Level 2 but very useful.

● Target setting

Based on your self-evaluation, decide on appropriate target(s). Be realistic and set achievable but challenging targets.

Target	Date for completion	Date achieved
e.g. Get a better understanding of mathematically similar shapes.		

Reflections on Chapter 10

- It is likely that some of the ideas in this chapter are more familiar to you than others.
- Think about those you use more in your personal life than as a teacher and vice versa.
- Any choreographers among you?

11 Handling data

This chapter will look at how data are collected, analysed and interpreted. We are presented with data in various forms every day, so we need to think carefully about how the data were collected in the first place, and how and why the information has been presented in a particular way and what the data tell us.

Tasks are designed to focus on both content knowledge and pedagogy, to be worked through collaboratively with your colleagues whenever possible. All the ideas presented here will transfer easily into your own setting and that of your learners.

By the end of this chapter you will understand:

- Collection of data.
- Analysis of data.
- Interpretation of data.

The minimum core standards for numeracy covered in this chapter are:

HD1 L2.1 L2.2 L2.3 L2.4

HD2 L2.1

Background information

Much is made of data in attempts to prove the success or otherwise of an event or activity. Earlier in this text we focused on the emphasis that Ofsted is now giving to data when making its decision about school and college performance.

Each year as the GCSE results are published a number of statements are made regarding the data that are provided through examination boards. In 2009 as quoted on the BBC website:

A* to C grades = 67.1% of whole.

A and A* grades = 21.6% of whole (up from 20.7% last year).

N Ireland A* to C = 75.1%

England A* to C = 66.9%

Wales A* to C = 65.5%

Overall pass rate (A* to G grades) = 98.6%

The results were illustrated by the chart shown in Figure 11.1.

This composite bar chart illustrates how the grades have been improving, and yet as teachers we often challenge the findings. Those involved will know that there are lots of factors which might impact on the data.

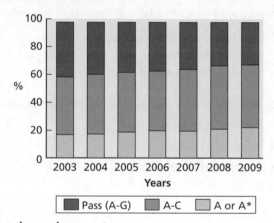

Figure 11.1 GCSE grades and pass rates
Source: Joint Council for Qualifications, www.jcq.uk. Used with permission

Sometimes data are used for political purposes. This could be the case here. You will be aware that there is no indication from this chart of the proportions of Bs, Cs, etc. More of a problem from a mathematical perspective is that there appears to be an error as the results from the three groups overlap according to the key. We cannot see the overlapping colours.

Figure 11.2 shows what 2009 would look like if the overlapping bars were separated out.

Governments trying to prove their policy has worked rely heavily on presenting data in a way which provides a positive message. Advertisers, too, rely on us reacting to data without really thinking about it. As one blogger put it:

The advert says 8 out of 10 cats prefer Whiskas. Who interviewed these cats and where are those cats now as we would like to speak to them?

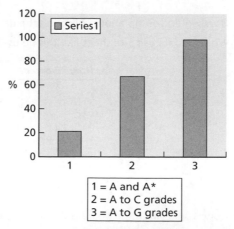

Figure 11.2 GCSE grades and pass rates (2009 in detail)

Data collection

Data can be collected in various ways: for example, by people with clipboards at supermarket doors, by telephone or by email survey. Data can be *quantitative* (for example, how much the person has just spent at the supermarket) or *qualitative* (for example, what they think of the new layout).

Numerical data can be *discrete* (for example, what size shoes are worn) or *continuous* (for example, the heights of a group of pre-school children). This matters because mathematically the data are analysed and presented in different ways.

The size of the *sample* also matters. Remembering the 2009 GCSE results, the sample was the whole *population* – in this case, everybody who sat GCSE that year – more than 600,000 individuals. The data in the form of grades are discrete. In most situations it is not possible to collect data from the whole population, so a representative sample is chosen.

> If you want to know more about sampling have a look at:
> **www.coventry.ac.uk/ec//~nhunt/meths/other.html**.

11

Much of the time, convenience samples are used as representative of the whole, although sometimes it is possible to use the whole population – for example, when analysing the examination results of one of your teaching groups. A stratified sample attempts to match the proportions in the population of girls, boys, different ages, etc.

Task 11.1

Ask five of your colleagues to think about when they last collected data to use in a teaching session. Find out what method they used to select the sample.

- How would you go about choosing your sample to find out how many hours students worked in paid employment while they were enrolled at college?

(continued)

● How would you go about collecting the data?

● Would a data capture sheet like this be useful?

Hours worked	Tally
2	///
3	//
4	///
5	/
6	
7	/

● How would you improve it? Is this any better?

Hours worked last week	Gender	Year of course
5	F	2
7	M	1
8	M	2
5	F	2

The timing of the work hours might make a difference.

● How could you change your data collection sheet to capture this information?

Think about Task 11.1

What have you learnt by doing this task? Think about the different surveys you may ask your students to conduct and consider what guidance you might give them on data collection.

Analysing data

Mean, median and *mode* are terms you are probably familiar with, but here is a reminder of their meanings.

This is a list of the money spent on lunch by one college student over a period of 9 days:

£3.09

£2.99

£4.30

£3.67

£3.09

£2.51

£5.14

£3.09

£2.99

Rewriting the amounts in order gives us £3.09 as the **median** (middle one):

£2.51

£2.99

£2.99

£3.09

£3.09

£3.09

£3.67

£4.30

£5.14

> If you are interested, you can find out how you could present these data as a box and whisker diagram:
>
> **www.tda.gov.uk/skillstests/numeracy/practicematerials/areascovered/boxwhiskerdiagrams.aspx**.

It also shows us that £3.09 is the **mode** as it occurs most often. Perhaps the student liked a particular combination of food and drink or perhaps many items are similarly priced. The **mean** (or average) is £3.43, which you work out by adding up the amounts spent £30.87 and dividing by 9, the number of days on which he had lunch.

The **range** is £5.14 − £2.51 = £2.63

Over a longer period of time it would become cumbersome to list each amount separately, so grouping the data would help.

Money spent in pounds	How many days: frequency	Mid value	Mid value × frequency
0–£1.99	4	0.995	3.98
£2.00–£2.49	23	1.245	28.635
£2.50–£2.99	30	2.745	82.35
£3.00–£3.49	35	3.245	113.575
£3.50–£3.99	12	3.745	56.94
£4.00–£5.00	6	4.50	27.00

By multiplying the number of days by the average in that row and adding these totals up, we get a reasonable estimate of what he spent. Dividing by the total number of days provides an estimate of the mean, £3.12.

As you can see, the approach is much less time consuming than adding up 100 individually listed numbers. If you want to know more about grouped data or how to draw a cumulative frequency curve, look at the BBC bitesize website.

You and your students will be presented with data which have already been analysed and presented in various forms, like the pie chart in Figure 11.3 which shows the pattern of electricity usage of one family.

● Is this typical of most households, do you think?

● How do you think these data were collected?

11

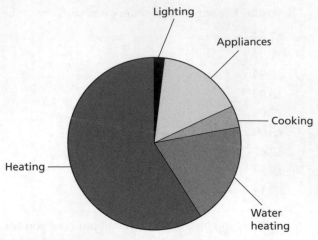

Figure 11.3 Pie chart showing use of electricity

Graphs can show the **correlation** between two variables like the example shown in Figure 11.4 which illustrates (not surprisingly) that, in general, heavier cars use more petrol. It is possible to calculate a coefficient that indicates how closely the two variables (weight and consumption) are related.

If you would like to know more about correlation go to:

www.bbc.co.uk/schools/gcsebitesize/maths/data/scatterdiagramsrev4.shtml.

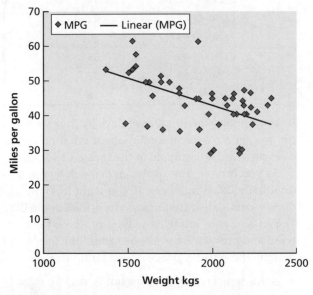

Figure 11.4 Correlation

Task 11.2

The Pepperoni Pizza

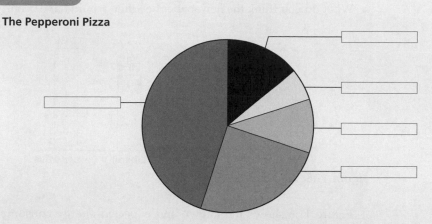

This pie chart shows the fraction of a 2 kg (very large!) pepperoni pizza (by weight) made up of each of the main components: crust 0.9 kg, cheese 500 g, pepperoni 200 g, tomato sauce 280 g, mushrooms 120 g.

- Can you label the diagram?
- Make a rough diagram of what the pie chart would look like if you broke the crust down into ingredients, flour, sugar, etc.
- Find a pizza recipe and have a go at constructing your own pie chart.
- Find menus for takeaway pizza companies.
- Does it look as if there's a correlation between size and price of a deep-pan Margherita pizza? You will need at least ten menus for comparison. Set a similar task for your learners.

Think about Task 11.2

- *Has thinking about the proportions changed your attitude to pizza eating?*
- *Is there a pizza delivery firm that offers particularly good or particularly bad value?*
- *Is there a topic you teach to which students have an entrenched attitude?*
- *Is there a way in which numeracy and statistics in particular could help them to consider a wider range of possibilities?*

Interpretation of data

Figure 11.5 (overleaf) illustrates again how data can be used to tell a particular story. By not drawing bar charts to scale or by not starting at zero the wrong inference can be drawn from the data.

The 4 per cent difference between Labour and Liberal is drawn to look proportionately bigger than the 10 per cent difference between Liberal and Conservative.

- Which party in the May 2010 elections is likely to have produced such a diagram?
- What do you think the newspaper headline would have been?

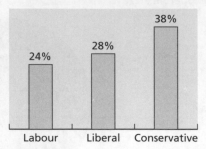

Figure 11.5 Who overtakes whom?

Figure 11.6 shows the known and expected energy consumption until 2030. Bar charts like this at first glance look very convincing, but there is no information on the way in which future energy use has been predicted.

The pictogram shown in Figure 11.7 gives the impression that roughly the same number of people travel by car as by bus, whereas in fact it is 40 compared with about 25. Most students walk, although it is not possible to state exactly whether it is 47 or 48.

The pictogram would be improved by making the symbols the same size and lining them up. A traditional bar chart might be less attractive but could provide more accurate information.

Task 11.3

Have a look at a newspaper or magazine. A trade magazine would give you useful material for using with your learners.

- Can you find evidence of where data have been used to try and persuade you to purchase the product?
- Can you find an example where the data have been presented in a misleading way?

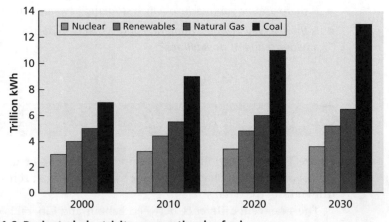

Figure 11.6 Projected electricity generation by fuel

Key

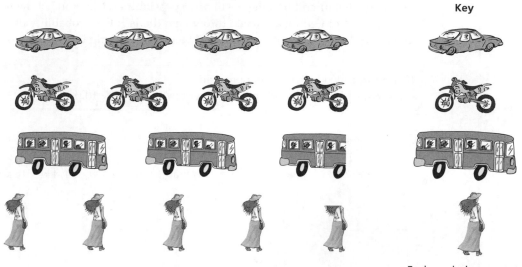

Each symbol represents
10 students

Figure 11.7 A pictogram

Think about Task 11.3

● *If you talked with your learners about this aspect of numeracy, do you think that they would consider that they were 'doing maths' when looking at misleading data?*

● *Would this give you an opportunity to discuss with them that mathematics is about more than getting the right answer to a problem presented on a worksheet?*

Probability

When something is certain to happen we give it a probability of 1. If it is certain not to happen, the probability is zero, while 50/50 is represented by a probability of $\frac{1}{2}$. The probability of a baby being a girl is approximately $\frac{1}{2}$.

The probability of three girls in a family is $\frac{1}{2} \times \frac{1}{2} \times \frac{1}{2} = \frac{1}{8}$. We can see that this is correct by listing all possibilities:

GGG

GBB

BGB

BBG

BGG

GGB

GBG

BBB

and noting that just one of the eight is what we are interested in. There are three ways that a family of three can consist of two boys and a girl, so the probability is $\frac{3}{8}$.

11

If there are four children there will be 16 possibilities. Can you list them?

The chance of getting a 6 when throwing a die is $\frac{1}{6}$: the probability of winning the lottery is $\frac{1}{14000000}$ so it is not surprising that we are not living in luxury!

> If you interested in knowing more read:
> **www.cimt.plymouth.ac.uk/projects/mepres/book8/bk8_10.pdf**.

Task 11.4

These are two fair spinners, which means that the arrow is equally likely to stop in any sector.

 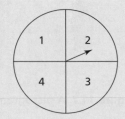

Complete this table to work out the probability of a total score that is a multiple of 3 (3, 6, 9, etc.)

+	1	2	3	4	5	6	7	8
1	2							
2		4						
3								11
4					9			

Think about Task 11.4

● *Would you have been able to work out this probability without completing every addition? If so how would you have decided what to do?*

Test yourself

Try these questions and check your answers. Use these questions to help you decide what should go in your action plan.

1 These are the ingredients for a microwaveable mushroom risotto: rice 28%, mushroom 25%, cream 16%, water, hard cheese, onion, white wine, each 5%, shiitake mushrooms 3.5%, oyster mushrooms 3.5%, butter 2% flavourings 2%.

 Draw a pie chart to show these proportions.

2 This bar chart shows the results of asking a group of students how many times a week they wash their hair.

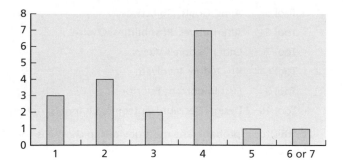

- How many students were asked?
- What is the modal number of times?
- What would be the median?
- Can you work out the mean if six times a week was actually the maximum number of washes?

3 The following statistics suggest that 17-year-olds are safer drivers than people in their twenties, and that those into their seventies are very safe.

Is this true? The vertical axis is the number of drivers involved in fatalities measured in thousands.

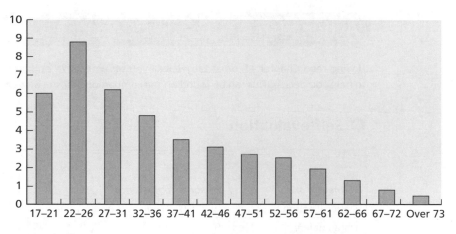

4 What is the probability of selecting a red card from a shuffled pack?

Going further

- Throughout this chapter you have been asked to think about, consider, interpret, etc. De Bono in his book *Lateral Thinking* (1965) suggests some thinking tools which can support this process. The ten Direct Attention Thinking Tools (DAT Ts) are:

  Tool 1   Consequences and Sequels.

  Tool 2   Plus, Minus, Interesting.

  Tool 3   Recognise, Analyse, Divide.

  Tool 4   Consider All Factors.

Tool 5   Aims, Goals, Objectives.

Tool 6   Alternatives, Possibilities, Choice.

Tool 7   Other People's Views.

Tool 8   Key Values Involved.

Tool 9   First Important Priorities.

Tool 10   Design/Decision, Outcome, Channels, Action.

For this topic probably the most obvious to choose is Tool 4, Consider All Factors, but others can be equally useful. Try using a DATT.

- The National Centre for Excellence in Teaching Mathematics has some suggestions for learning maths outside the classroom on **www.ncetm.org.uk/resources/9272** reporting on a study on leaf size. NCETM also describes how a quantity can be estimated through sampling on **www.ncetm.org.uk/resources/9709**. Have a look.

- Watch a Teachers TV programme on correlation: *Tick or trash – are cabbies brains bigger?* See: **www.teachers.tv/video/1851**.

- Try this quiz on Skillwise at **www.bbc.co.uk/apps/ifl/skillswise/mod_quizzes/numbers/ handlingdata/probability/quizengine** or, if you are less confident, have a look at the factsheets on the same website.

Action plan

Having read Chapter 11, what targets will you set yourself? Complete the self-evaluation grid to help you decide. This can be found on the companion website at **www.pearsoned.co.uk/qtls**.

● Self-evaluation

Numeracy skill	Personal competence			Confident in providing opportunities for learners to use this skill		
Data collection	High (H)	Medium (M)	Low (L)	H	M	L
Data analysis	H	M	L	H	M	L
Data interpretation	H	M	L	H	M	L
Probability	H	M	L	H	M	L

● Target setting

Based on your self-evaluation, decide on appropriate target(s). Be realistic and set achievable but challenging targets.

Target	Date for completion	Date achieved
e.g. Improve my understanding of probability		

Reflections on Chapter 11

- If you had given your knowledge and understanding of data handling a rating at the beginning of this chapter, what would it have been if 5 meant that you felt very confident and 1 that you felt very unsure?

- What would it be now? Think about what skills you already had that you were not aware were useful in this area of mathematics.

- Think about when you used these skills in your daily life, choosing a holiday or planning a diet without appreciating how many numerical processes you were employing.

11

12 ICT and numeracy

It is only in the last 20 or so years that computers have been used to support learning. Up until that time it was a rare event for numeracy skills to be taught or assessed in a computer room. In addition, few learners had access at home. Today learners of all ages live lives surrounded by technology, and there is a wealth of material available to support the teaching of number competence. As a result there is much to cover in a chapter. Our approach here has been to refer back to previous skills and knowledge covered in previous chapters and demonstrate just how ICT might be used.

This chapter includes these topics from:

- Chapter 7
  - Pascal's triangle
  - Number lines
  - Equivalence of fractions, decimals and percentages
- Chapter 9
  - Spreadsheets to convert currencies, temperatures, etc.
- Chapter 10
  - Transformations
- Chapter 11
  - Analysing and presenting data.

First, think about the technology you have access to.

Task 12.1

Create a table similar to that below of technology and classify it according to availability, and also your level of confidence and whether or not you think that you could use it for developing numeracy in your learners.

Technology	Availability	Confidence	Possible uses
Interactive whiteboards			
Internet access			
Electronic calculator			

- Ideas you might add include DVDs, televisions, social media, e.g. blogging/Twitter, hand-held voting devices, etc.
- How frequently do you currently use technology to enhance your lesson planning?

Think about Task 12.1

- *Are you surprised by the length of your list?*
- *Are there more opportunities than you previously considered?*
- *How could you become more confident in the use of less familiar technologies?*

How technology could be used in support

Here we return to content from earlier chapters to consider how technology could be used in support.

● Chapter 7 Mental and written strategies

Using Pascal's work, students like to generate the triangle and are intrigued by the patterns produced by shading numbers with different properties, e.g. multiples of 4. However, this can take up valuable lesson time unless you use some of the many interactive websites. One you may like to use is the National Library of Virtual Manipulatives (NLVM) which can be downloaded and used for a very wide range of interactive activities including work on Pascal's triangle. Completed diagrams may be saved or printed. The same site includes number line work, whole numbers and fractions as well as a host of other interactive and fun tasks in all areas of mathematics.

Using a whiteboard on screen, number lines can be divided into different fractions and then overlaid to show equivalence:

$0 \underline{\hspace{10cm}} 1$

$\dfrac{0}{2} \underline{\hspace{6cm}} \dfrac{1}{2} \underline{\hspace{6cm}} \dfrac{2}{2}$

$\dfrac{0}{4} \underline{\hspace{2.5cm}} \dfrac{1}{4} \underline{\hspace{2.5cm}} \dfrac{2}{4} \underline{\hspace{2.5cm}} \dfrac{3}{4} \underline{\hspace{2.5cm}} \dfrac{4}{4}$

$\dfrac{0}{8} \quad \dfrac{1}{8} \quad \dfrac{2}{8} \quad \dfrac{3}{8} \quad \dfrac{4}{8} \quad \dfrac{5}{8} \quad \dfrac{6}{8} \quad \dfrac{7}{8} \quad \dfrac{8}{8}$

Another use of technology associated with the learning in this chapter might be the use of the whiteboard to sort data. If a set of similar data is provided the students can move the numbers around so that eventually equivalent fractions, decimals and perhaps percentages are grouped together.

● Chapter 9 Common measures

In this chapter tasks were set that required the transformation of one measurement to another. To achieve this electronically it is possible to use the formula function on an Excel® spreadsheet. Learners need to know how to write the formula, remembering to include the brackets, but the spreadsheet can then be used repeatedly to convert from one measure to another, avoiding repetitive calculations. Internet sites which convert from pounds to dollars or metres to yards will all be using this principle.

Task 12.2

Think about working with your learners to produce a subject-specific set of conversion spreadsheets. The spreadsheet can then be used to produce a conversion graph.

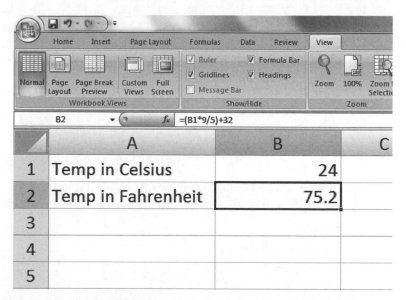

Figure 12.1 An Excel spreadsheet
Source: Microsoft product screenshot reprinted with permission from Microsoft Corporation

● Chapter 9 Shape and space

Shapes available in most Windows® packages as part of the toolbar function make it possible for learners to create tessellations with relative ease.

For example, if we take a regular hexagon:

Copy it:

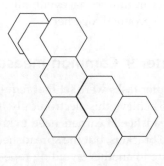

Then move the shapes to show they tessellate. You can use the grouping function to create shapes made of multiple shapes. For example:

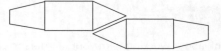

Rotations and reflections can also be demonstrated using the same software:

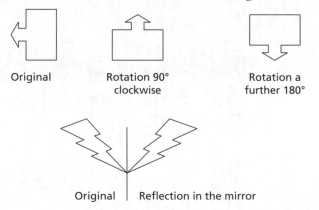

Original   Rotation 90°   Rotation a
clockwise   further 180°

Original | Reflection in the mirror

If you wanted to use something more sophisticated then you can find out about sample packages from www.ncetm.org.uk/mathemapedia/Dynamic%20Geometry.

- Cabri
- Geometer Sketchpad
- Geogebra
- Cinderella
- TI-nspire
- Cabri Junior for the TI-84

These are a just a few possibilities, all of which use a click, grab and drag approach enabling learners to manipulate shapes.

● Chapter 11 Data handling

An Excel spreadsheet can be used to create bar charts and pie charts as illustrated below. Figure 12.2 – a bar chart – illustrates Task 11.1 from Chapter 11. The spreadsheet can also be used to calculate the mean. (Can you show what the mean is?)

Figure 12.3 is a pie chart generated by using data on the food categories present in a pizza.

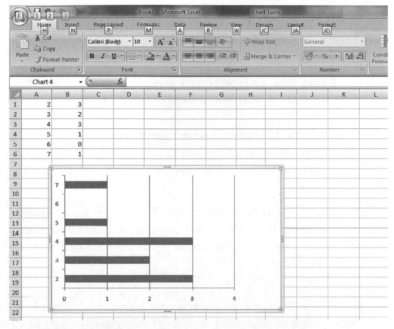

Figure 12.2 An Excel bar chart

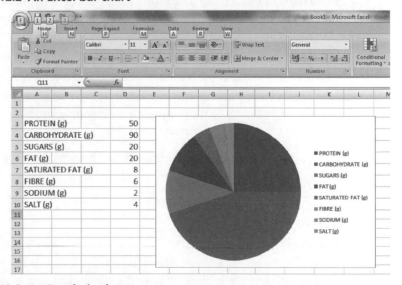

Figure 12.3 An Excel pie chart

Source: Microsoft product screenshots reprinted with permission from Microsoft Corporation

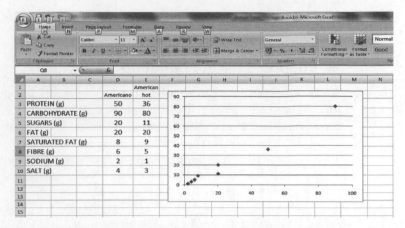

Figure 12.4 An Excel scatter graph
Source: Microsoft product screenshot reprinted with permission from Microsoft Corporation

Figure 12.4 shows a scatter graph comparing the protein, sugars, etc. of two pizzas, which can easily be produced.

The skills acquired are transferable into a range of settings.

In addition there are resources including lesson plans on the National Strategies website: **http://nationalstrategies.standards.dcsf.gov.uk/node/96367?uc=force_uj** including data on Kendal and Cambridge weather over a number of years to allow hypotheses to be tested.

If you want to encourage your learners to collect their own data, there are several online questionnaire-generating tools such as Survey Monkey. Interactive tools such as these make it much more interesting for the student to produce questionnaires and for others to complete them. The software will also analyse responses, allowing for quick processing and therefore providing more discussion opportunities to consider both the questions asked and the responses obtained.

Probability experiments can be undertaken by using simulations such as those on **www.mathsonline.co.uk/nonmembers/resource/prob/**.

Within a very short space of time I had 'thrown' three coins 600 times achieving:

71   head head head

227   head head tail (in any order)

218   head tail tail (in any order)

84   tail tail tail

These results are close to the theoretical frequencies of 75, 225, 225, 75. It is useful to encourage students to look at how the theoretical and experimental values become closer as the number of trials increases.

Of course, it is possible physically to throw the three coins and to use an Excel® spreadsheet to record results, but it is much slower and noisier!

If you have downloaded NLVM, it has some interactive spinners as well as coin tossing.

Going further

- Read the Becta report on the impact of the use of ICT in educational institutions. There is a section specific to mathematics at: **http://partners.becta.org.uk/page_documents/ research/impact_ict_schools.pdf**.
- Read about selecting tasks on: **www.ncetm.org.uk/mathemapedia/Selecting%20 Suitable%20Learning%20Activities%20(at%20key%20stage%203)**.
- Find out how colleagues in other subject areas use technology to enhance their lessons.

Action plan

- Look back at Task 12.1 and consider if there now seem to be more opportunities than you previously thought.
- Make the decision to try something different tomorrow!

And finally...

This book has been designed with a number of audiences in mind. We hope you will find it a useful addition to your professional development whether you are in training, training the trainers or using the ideas presented here to refresh your skills as a well-established educator.

We have enjoyed working together to produce this text, have learned much from each other in this collaborative venture and look forward to receiving your comments and feedback as we visit the many organisations we hope will use and benefit from our work.

Liz and Anne

12

Appendix Cooperative group work

You will no doubt have used group work on many occasions and will have found that the learning is frequently deeper than that achieved through whole-class teaching. Cooperative group work develops the process further so that each group has responsibility for one particular aspect of a larger task. Roles are allocated to individuals and to groups, and in many ways the process mirrors what happens in the real world. Plumbers do not need to be expert plasterers, but it is useful if they have some understanding of the skills required. Cooperative group work requires learners to use their communication skills to the full to explain their knowledge and understanding to others: hairdressers must be able to explain to clients what the treatment entails, and mechanics to the car owner as to why the MOT has not been passed.

The number of groups is obviously dependent on the class size and, although it is theoretically possible to have a group of one, the minimum number to allow for useful discussion is two. The groups should vary in make-up on different occasions so that students learn to work in different ways with different people with differing strengths in numeracy. Of course, this approach is equally useful regardless of the topic, but in all situations the main task is preceded by subtasks which vary in number but are usually three or four.

So, supposing there are three subtasks and 12 learners in your class. Students will be allocated to three groups of four and each will work on one subtask.

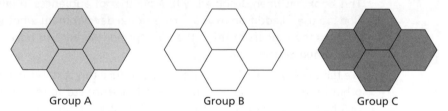

Group A   Group B   Group C

Each group member is responsible for making sure that everyone in that group becomes expert on that particular subtask. If subtask A is finding the area of rectangles, then everyone in that group must be able to do so. The allocation of subtasks offers a means of differentiating: subtask C might be finding the surface area of a cylinder, for example.

Each expert group is then reformed to create two or four new groups, each with experts on all three subtasks in readiness to undertake the main task.

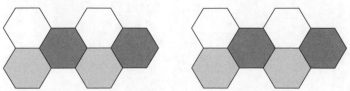

The intention is that each individual brings a particular expertise essential to the completion of the main task. All can contribute and all feel confident to do so as a result of the subtask activity.

A suitable task for three subgroups is suggested below.

● Main task

This is not seen by the students until expertise has been acquired on the subtasks.

> Suppose a family wishes to build a swimming pool in their garden.
> - They have identified two possibilities, one of which is a rectangle 10m wide by 15m long which slopes from a depth of 1m at one end to 2m at the other.
> - The second pool is also 10m wide but is 18m long with semicircular ends. It is a constant depth of 1.5m.
> - Both have vertical sides.
>
> Draw plans and elevations to show what the preformed pools would look like from above and from each of the sides, before being put into the ground. You will also need to calculate the volume of water in each pool assuming that the water level is 20cm below the top edge.
>
> The pool sides and floor will need to be kept algae free, so you will need to calculate this area; and also the heat loss depends on the surface area of the pool.
> - Which pool would your group choose and why?
> - You must include some of your findings when explaining your decision.

These are suggestions for subtasks which can be in the form of specific questions if this is preferred.

● Subtasks

Group A Find out about trapeziums

Group B Find out about cylinders

Group C Find out about plans and elevations

The subtasks may be allocated according to difficulty or in an attempt to bridge a gap in understanding, but whatever is set has to be within the capabilities of the group. Remember that they are supported by each other as well as by yourself.

Answers

Chapter 1

Number workout
1.1 10,100,1000
1.2 29,102,98
1.3 45,60,94

Chapter 2

Number workout
2.1 40,900,9000
2.2 165,720,714
2.3 504,912,2010

Chapter 3

Number workout
3.1

2	4	1	3
1	3	4	2
4	2	3	1
3	1	2	4

3.2 The original number is doubled and then 12 added so halving means we have the original number plus 6. When we take away the original number we are always left with 6.
3.3 3 + 9 = 12
12 + 16 = 28 the top number.
3.4 The smallest number whole number with three digits is 100.
1,000,000,000 is a thousand million.
3.5 a. 4 × 5 × 3 = 20 × 3 = 60
b. 7 × 9 × 4 = 63 × 4 = 252

Chapter 4

Number workout
4.1 7,9,201
4.2 707,302,261
4.3 30650,2121,818

Chapter 5

Number workout
5.1 49,99,217
5.2 91,630,954
5.3 2349,2961,7497

Chapter 7

Task 7.1
Prime factors of 24 are $2 \times 2 \times 2 \times 3$
Of 240 are $2 \times 2 \times 2 \times 2 \times 3 \times 5$
4800 are $2 \times 2 \times 2 \times 2 \times 2 \times 2 \times 3 \times 5 \times 5$

Test yourself

2.1×39	81.9
$-3 \times -2 + 1$	7
$452 \div 90$	5.02
$2 \times 3 - 5.1$	0.9
$1.4 + 3.5$	4.9
$15 \div 2$	7.5
$1\frac{3}{4} + 4\frac{1}{4}$	6
$5\frac{1}{3} \times \frac{3}{8}$	2

$81.9 - 0.9 = 81$, which is a square number.

Chapter 8

Task 8.2
Ideal   Just overweight   About 10 kg

Test yourself
1   Estimate $1.5 - 0.16 \times 10 = -0.1$ Exact -0.0924 Other estimates possible
2   Estimate $4^2 - 5 = 16 - 5 = 11$ Exact 10.41
   a. £286.55   **b.** 286.52

Chapter 9

Task 9.2
Jan 11th, Jan 12th

Task 9.3
4.063 km

Task 9.4
B
166.9   200.25   66.9

Test yourself

At 2 pm Jo went to fill up her car with petrol. The price per litre was £1.10 but as the tank had a capacity of 35 litres it was quite an expensive trip. She decided that she needed a few bits and pieces so bought 500 grammes of butter, a 370 gramme jar of jam and a loaf of bread.

The garage was only 2 miles/km from home but it was a slow journey back taking 20 minutes. She worked out that her average speed was only 6 miles/km per hour.

5 minutes after getting home at 1455 hours Jo sat down to her afternoon snack. Well, at least I was only at the garage for 55 minutes, she thought.

Chapter 10

Test yourself

1

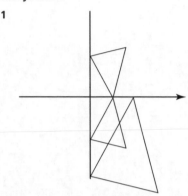

2 Centimetres, metres
Surface area 50 squared units, volume 187.5 cubic units
3 216.3 cm
4 6

Chapter 11

Task 11.4

+	1	2	3	4	5	6	7	8
1	2	3	4	5	6	7	8	9
2	3	4	5	6	7	8	9	10
3	4	5	6	7	8	9	10	11
4	5	6	7	8	9	10	11	12

Probability 11/32

Test yourself

1

2   18,4, 3.5, 3.1
3   No because it does not reflect the number of drivers in each age group.
4   ½

Glossary

Academic Focusing on the acquisition of facts, information and abstract theoretical, rather than practical, knowledge.

Analysis The breaking-down of complex situations and arguments into many related points in order to examine the relationship between these parts.

Application Application, in academic language, refers to the ability to use knowledge and understanding in different situations.

Area of learning A subject or topic within a specified field of knowledge.

Assessment for learning Judgements used to support teaching and learning, monitor learners' progress and illuminate their strengths and weaknesses, also known as formative assessment/judgement.

Brainstorming Putting together a small group of learners to produce a large number of creative ideas in a short time for subsequent evaluation. Also known as 'word storming', this activity can take place on an individual basis.

Buzz group A small group of learners who spend a few minutes discussing an idea or thought-provoking question among themselves.

Change agent Any member of staff who is engaged in enabling and facilitating change in practice within their organisation.

Common knowledge, skills and attributes (CKSA) The knowledge, skills and attributes that all young people need for learning, employment and adult life. For example, personal awareness, problem solving, moral and ethical awareness. CKSA forms part of the **Core**.

Communities of practice Groups of individuals sharing common beliefs and values who group together to share and develop practice.

Complementary learning Learning related to the focus of a learner's **main learning**, such as Latin for a learner with a modern foreign languages focus. It may contribute towards achievement of the **threshold** or be additional to it.

Component The building blocks for the proposed diploma system. A discrete subject or **area of learning** with its own assessment arrangements, achievement in which gives credit towards the award of a **diploma**. Components will build on existing qualifications, such as GCSEs and A levels and other existing qualifications.

Comprehension or understanding in academic terms requires not just the mere recall of information, but insight into the ways in which the information may have been derived or how it relates to other information available on the topic.

Continuing professional development (CPD) Sometimes referred to as 'staff development'. Any activity that helps teachers/tutors/trainers maintain, improve or broaden their knowledge, understanding and skills, and become more effective in their role.

146

Cooperative learning A strategy in which small groups, each with students with different abilities, use various learning activities to improve their understanding of a subject. Each member of a group is responsible not only for learning what is taught but also for helping fellow learners learn, thus creating an atmosphere of achievement.

Core (learning) Skills, knowledge and experiences common to and required for the achievement of all **diplomas: functional literacy and communication; functional mathematics; functional ICT; extended project; CKSA; personal review, planning and guidance**; and an entitlement to **wider activities**.

Credit Value ascribed to a **component** based on a measure of notional learning time. Nothing smaller than a component can provide credit towards a **diploma**.

Critical analysis The ability to break down complex situations and arguments and to assess objectively the implications for one's practice.

Critical incident An episode of teaching, a single session or one event during a session that is subjected by the teacher to close analysis by means of reflection in order to develop their practice.

Critique To critically examine something, such as a session plan, to give feedback, to recognise strengths and suggest strategies for improvement.

Deep learning A term used to describe learning that is committed to the permanent memory, as opposed to **surface learning** which is retained for as long as is needed and then discarded.

Diagnostic assessment Assessment which gives in-depth information about an individual's strengths and weaknesses in relation to literacy, language and numeracy, enabling tutors to design a **programme** of work specifically to meet the needs of the learner.

Differentiation Identifying and addressing the different needs, interests and abilities of all learners to give them the best possible chance of achieving their learning goals.

Diploma Proposed qualification recognising achievement in a **programme** that meets **threshold** requirements for **core** and **main learning**.

E-learning The generic term for learning facilitated and supported through the use of information and communications technology. It may involve the use of, for example, computers, interactive whiteboards, digital cameras, the internet, the institutional intranet, virtual learning environments and electronic communication tools such as email, bulletin boards, chat facilities and video conferencing.

End user Ultimate beneficiaries of the 14–19 education and training system, especially higher education and employers.

Evaluation The skill of making judgements based on a clear assessment of the available evidence; also, specifically, the process whereby learners, teachers/tutors/trainers or an organisation evaluate perceptions of a learning experience, a study programme or a particular course or activity. Evaluation is usually part of a formative process aimed at improving standards. It may be carried out by questionnaire or by interviews.

Extended project A significant autonomous piece of work completed by each learner as part of their **core learning**. Completing the extended project would require learners to develop and demonstrate a range of skills such as planning, research and problem solving. The final outcome would be dependent on the nature of the project selected by the learner. It might be a written report, but could also be a piece of artwork, a construction or a performance.

Extension activities Additional activities provided for learners who have completed basic learning tasks. The activities should be more complex and challenging than the ones that have gone before, thus supporting the development of talented learners.

Formative assessment/judgement *See* **Assessment for learning**.

Functional ICT The ICT skills that young people need to function as informed citizens and effective learners and in the workplace. A **component** of the **core**.

Functional literacy and communication The literacy and communication skills that young people need to function as informed citizens and effective learners and in the workplace. A **component** of the **core**.

Functional mathematics The mathematical skills young people need to function as informed citizens and effective learners and in the workplace. A **component** of the **core**.

GCE General Certificate of Education or A levels – an advanced-level general qualification.

GNVQ General National Vocational Qualifications – intermediate and foundation-level qualifications covering broad vocational sectors, such as health and social care. They are in the process of being withdrawn.

In-course assessment Work set and marked by teachers over the duration of the course that contributes to the award of a grade in a subject or **area of learning**.

Individual review A formative **assessment** that encourages learners, either on an individual basis or as part of a group, to evaluate their progress in a given task or programme and to plan and set targets for the next stage of development.

Individualisation Recognising and responding to individual needs.

Initial assessment The process of recognising individual learners' needs, aptitudes, preferences and prior learning in order to plan and provide an appropriate learning programme to meet those needs.

Kinaesthetic Practical or tactile approach to learning using the sense of touch.

Knowledge The information and experience that a learner has acquired or learned and is able to recall or use in a given situation or activity.

Learning cycle A process identified by Kolb, whereby the experience of trying something new is followed by reflection and evaluation. The process is cyclical and can be iterative and is thought to be central to the way individuals learn and develop.

Learning outcomes Statements indicating what a learner should know or be able to do at the end of a given period.

Learning preferences The way a learner likes to be engaged in the process of learning, whether it be through the use of computers, self-study, or through visual, kinaesthetic or practical activities.

Learning styles inventory A diagnostic instrument used to help individuals assess their preferred approach to learning.

Level Demand or difficulty of a qualification, **programme** or **component**.

Lines (of learning) Related subjects or **areas of learning**. **Programmes** and **diplomas** will be based on one of a number of lines.

Main learning Learning chosen by the learner which constitutes the bulk of each **diploma**. It should ensure achievement and progression within individual subjects and **areas of learning**.

Mindmap A diagram which summarises information or ideas, with linkages drawn between ideas and themes.

Moderation A process of checking a sample of assessed work for the consistency of marking and to arrive at a grade for work. Moderation is carried out by examiners other than those involved in the original marking.

Objectives Precise and measurable statements describing what the teacher/tutor/trainer intends that learners should achieve in a specified period.

Pathway A progression route through the **diploma** framework.

Pedagogy The theory of learning. Tried and tested ideas about how best to organise episodes of learning, i.e. theoretical and procedural knowledge about teaching.

Peer assessment Using learners to check each other's work, applying clear criteria to make judgements to support the learning of others and themselves.

Personal review, planning and guidance Support for the young person to understand themself as a learner and how the different parts of their **programme** relate to one another, and to identify their learning and career goals and how to achieve them.

Programme Overarching term for a combination of **components** followed by a learner or group of learners. Programmes may differ in content, **volume**, **level** and length, but share the characteristic of bringing components together into a whole. Achievement in a programme should be recognised by the award of a **diploma**, provided that **threshold** requirements are met. A programme may be bigger than a diploma, and additional achievement beyond the required threshold should be recorded on a **transcript**.

RARPA Recognising and recording progress and achievement in non-accredited learning. This is an approach to measure learners' success in non-accredited learning. There is some debate about extending this approach to measure improvements made in adult education environments.

Reflection The process whereby a learner (teacher/tutor/trainer) takes time to consider a given learning experience with a view to making changes in order to continuously improve their approach to learning or their practice.

Resource-based learning An approach to learning which often involves a specific area or designated learning environment where individuals use a range of resources (computers, books, journals) to carry out set tasks.

Resources Discovery Network (RDN) A free national gateway to internet resources for the learning, teaching and research community.

Screening A process that indicates, following an initial assessment, the likelihood that a learner has support needs over and above those normally required to complete a programme of study.

Self-assessment The type of assessment undertaken by the learner (the teacher/tutor/trainer) to evaluate their performance, strengths and weaknesses.

Self-awareness Implies an understanding of the individual's strengths and weaknesses, the ability to identify learning goals and areas for improvement.

SMART Objectives that are specific, measurable, achievable, realistic (or relevant) and time bound.

Strategic learning An approach to learning which sees knowledge as a means to an end (such as passing an examination). In such cases the learner selects the knowledge they need to retain and consciously commits it to their short-term memory purely for the purposes for which it is initially intended.

Study skills The skills needed by learners in order to successfully participate in or complete a programme of study. They may include note taking, researching information, time management, essay writing.

Subject pedagogy Accepted good practice, underpinned by theory, in designing teaching/training episodes associated with a specific area of the curriculum.

Summative assessment The final evaluation point, used at the end of a unit, module or programme, to assess a learner's attainment of that unit of learning.

Surface learning Learning which is retained in the consciousness on a short-term basis, for practical application, to be discarded once it has been utilised.

Synthesis The ability to bring a number of issues together and describe links and associations that make this link possible. Linking theory to support the findings of your own research requires the skill of synthesis.

Teacher(-led) assessment *See* **In-course assessment**.

Threshold The minimum **level** and **volume** of achievement in **core** and **main learning** required for the award of a diploma.

Transcript Document providing details of the **components** that constitute a learner's **programme** and achievement in them. This includes non-assessed activities such as **CKSA** and **wider activities**, and achievement beyond the **threshold** required for award of a **diploma**.

Triads Groups of three learners working together.

Understanding The learner shows the capacity to use the current knowledge, concepts and skills to solve a problem or task or to answer specific questions concerning that topic.

Unit Block of teaching and learning within a **component**. Units may be separately assessed but do not on their own provide **credit** towards a **diploma**.

Vocational learning Learning which develops the knowledge, skills and attributes directly relevant to the workplace in general or a job in particular. It is usually practical or applied, rather than abstract or theoretical.

Volume A measure of the amount of work required.

Wider activities Tasks set for learners to complete to demonstrate additional and/or more developed skill.

Work-based learning Learning which takes place predominantly on the job rather than in structured learning settings.

Bibliography

Armitage, A., Bryant, R., Dunnill, R., Hayes, D., Hudson, A., Kent, J., Lawes, S., Renwick, M. (2009) *Teaching and Training in Post-Compulsory Education*, Buckingham: OUP

Balderstone, D. and Lambert, D. (2000) *Learning to Teach Geography in Secondary Schools*, London: Routledge Farmer

Blackstone, T. (2000) *Prison Education*, London: Fabian Society

Brittan, J. (1996) *An Introduction to Numeracy Teaching*, London: BSA

Bynner, J. and Parsons, S. (2006) *New Light on Literacy and Numeracy*, London: National Research and Development Centre for Adult Literacy and Numeracy

Cameron, D. (2000) *Good to Talk? Living and working in a communication culture*, London: Sage

Carter, R. and Nunan, D. (eds) (2001) *The Cambridge Guide to Teaching English to Speakers of Other Languages*, Cambridge: CUP

Casey, B. and Davidson, M. (2006) *Numeracy in a Vocational Context*, London: National Research and Development Centre for Adult Literacy and Numeracy

Chinn, S.J. (2004) *The trouble with maths, A practical guide to helping learners with numeracy difficulties*, London: Routledge

Crystal, D. (2003) *The Cambridge Encyclopedia of the English Language*, (2nd edn), Cambridge: CUP

Crystal, D. (2004) *Making Sense of Grammar*, Harlow: Longman

Crystal, D. (2004) *Rediscover Grammar*, (3rd edn), Harlow: Longman.

Dench, S. and Regan, J. (2000) *Learning in Later Life: motivation and impact*, Institute of Employment Studies

Department for Education (2010) *Policy Exchange*. London: Her Majesty's Stationery Office

Department for Education and Skills (2000) *Skills for Life: The Moser Report*, London: Her Majesty's Stationery Office

Department for Education and Skills (2002) *Success for All*, London: Her Majesty's Stationery Office

Department for Education and Skills (2004) *Equipping our Teachers for the Future*, London: Her Majesty's Stationery Office

Department for Education and Skills (2005) *The Tomlinson Review of 14–19 Education*, London: Her Majesty's Stationery Office

Department for Education and Skills (2006) *The Leitch Review of Skills*, London: Her Majesty's Stationery Office

Department of Innovation, Universities and Skills (2007) *The Workforce Reform Review*, London: Her Majesty's Stationery Office

Department of Work and Pensions (2008) *Technology for Work*. London: Her Majesty's Stationery Office

Department of Work and Pensions (2009) *Beating the Recession*. London: Her Majesty's Stationery Office

Ekynsmith, C. and Bynner, J. (1994) *The basic skills of young adults: some findings from Britain, the 1970 cohort*, London: ALBSU

Felstead, J. (2009) *Improving Working as Learning*, London: Routledge

Flegg, G. (1984) *Numbers, their History and Meaning*, London: Andre Deutsch

Freeman, D. (2005) *Creating Emotion in Games*, Boston: London

Further Education National Training Organisation (2003) *Training in the Further Education Sector*, London: FENTO

Gorgorió, N. and de Abreu, G. (2009) 'Social representations as mediators of practice in mathematics classrooms with immigrant students', *Education Studies in Mathematics*, vol. 72, pp. 61–76

Hamilton, M. and Hillier, Y. (2006) *Changing Faces of Adult Literacy, Language and Numeracy*, Stoke-on-Trent: Trentham

Henderson, A. (1998) *Maths for the Dyslexic, A Practical Guide*, London: Fulton

Her Majesty's Stationery Office (1998) *The Blackstone Review of the Prison Education Service*, London: Her Majesty's Stationery Office

Her Majesty's Stationery Office (2004) *The State of the Nation: The National Audit Office Annual Report*, London: Her Majesty's Stationery Office

Herrington, M. and Kendall, A. (eds) (2005) *Insights from research and practice: A handbook for adult literacy, numeracy and ESOL practitioners*, Leicester: NIACE

Jenkins, A., Greenwood, C. and Vignoles, A. (2007) *Returns to qualifications in England*, London: OUP

Joyce, B., Calhourn, E. and Hopkins, D. (2008) *Models of Learning: Tools for Teaching*, Milton Keynes: OUP

Kadosh, M. (2005) *Biological influences in number proficiency*, London: NIACE

KPMG (2005) *The Economic Cost of Poor Numeracy Skills: Report for the Department of Universities and Skills*, London: Her Majesty's Stationery Office

Lave, J. (1988) *Cognition and Practice: mind, mathematics and culture in everyday life*, Cambridge: Cambridge University Press

LifeLong Learning UK (2008) *Consultation on the Professional Standards of Teachers in the Life-Long Learning Sector*, London: Her Majesty's Stationery Office

McGivney, V. (1990) *Education's for Other People*, Milton Keynes: NIACE

McIntosh, R. (2004) *Further analysis of returns to academic and vocational qualifications*, London: OUP

Office for European Community Development (2000) *Population Survey*.

Organisation for Economic Co-operation and Development (2007) *Employment Outlook*, London: Her Majesty's Stationery Office

PWC (2005) *The economic benefits of higher education qualifications*, London: Routledge

Reece, I. and Walker, S. (1999) *Teaching in the Further Education System*, Sunderland: Business Education

Swann, M. (2006) *Collaborative Learning in Mathematics, A challenge to our beliefs and practices*, Leicester: NIACE

Tett, L., Hamilton, M. and Hillier, Y. (2006) *Adult Literacy, Numeracy & Language: Policy, Practice and Research*, Maidenhead: McGraw-Hill

● Journals

Adult Learning
Numeracy Briefing
Reflect, The Magazine of the NRDC
Journal of Current Biology: March, 2007

● Websites

www.ncetm.org.uk The National Centre for Excellence in Teaching of Mathematics (NCETM)

www.lifelonglearninguk.org Lifelong Learning UK: Professional Standards for teachers of Mathematics (Numeracy)

www.Maths4Life Resource 'Thinking Through Mathematics, strategies for teaching and learning' DfES 2007

www.dfes.gov.uk/readwriteplus Adult Numeracy Core Curriculum and related documents

www.esolcitizenship.org.uk Citizenship Materials for ESOL learners

www.lifelonglearninguk.org Lifelong Learning UK: Professional Standards for teachers of ESOL (Literacy and Numeracy)

www.nrdc.org.uk National Research and Development Centre for Adult Literacy and Numeracy

www.dfes.gov.uk/readwriteplus ESOL Adult Core Curriculum, ESOL Access for All and related documents

www. theexcellencegateway.org.uk

www.dcsf.gov.uk

www.qcda.org.uk – accessed 1.07.09

www.ucas.org.uk – accessed 1.07.09

Index